THE HAMLYN LECTURES

FORTY-THIRD SERIES

INTRODUCING

A

EUROPEAN LEGAL ORDER

AUSTRALIA
The Law Book Company
Sydney

CANADA
The Carswell Company
Toronto, Ontario

INDIA
N.M. Tripathi (Private) Ltd.
Bombay
and
Eastern Law House (Private) Ltd.
Calcutta
M.P.P. House
Bangalore
Universal Book Traders
Delhi

ISRAEL
Steimatzky's Agency Ltd.
Tel-Aviv

PAKISTAN
Pakistan Law House
Karachi

INTRODUCING

A

EUROPEAN LEGAL ORDER

by

GORDON SLYNN

Published under the auspices of

THE HAMLYN TRUST

LONDON

STEVENS & SONS/SWEET & MAXWELL

1992

Published in 1992
by Stevens & Sons Ltd./Sweet & Maxwell Ltd.
South Quay Plaza, 183 Marsh Wall, London E14 9FT
Computerset by
PB Computer Typesetting, Pickering, N. Yorks.
Printed in Great Britain

A CIP catalogue record for this book
is available from the British Library

ISBN 0421463104
ISBN 0421473002 pbk

CONTENTS

The Hamlyn Lectures   vii
The Hamlyn Trust   xi

Preface   xiii
Introduction   xv

1. Establishing A Court   1

2. Effecting A Market   41

3. Affecting The People   85

4. Adapting To Change   136

    Closing Thought   173

Table of Cases   175
Table of Treaties   182
Index   184

THE HAMLYN LECTURES

1949   Freedom under the Law
         by the Rt. Hon. Lord Denning

1950   The Inheritance of the Common Law
         by Richard O'Sullivan, Esq.

1951   The Rational Strength of English Law
         by Professor F.H. Lawson

1952   English Law and the Moral Law
         by Professor A.L. Goodhart

1953   The Queen's Peace
         by Sir Carleton Kemp Allen

1954   Executive Discretion and Judicial Control
         by Professor C.J. Hamson

1955   The Proof of Guilt
         by Professor Clanville Williams

1956   Trial by Jury
         by the Rt. Hon. Lord Devlin

1957   Protection from Power under English Law
         by the Rt. Hon. Lord MacDermott

1958   The Sanctity of Contracts in English Law
         by Professor Sir David Hughes Parry

1959 Judge and Jurist in the Reign of Victoria
by C.H.S. Fifoot, Esq.

1960 The Common Law in India
by M.C. Setalvad, Esq.

1961 British Justice: The Scottish Contribution
by Professor Sir Thomas Smith

1962 Lawyer and Litigant in England
by the Rt. Hon. Sir Robert Megarry

1963 Crime and the Criminal Law
by the Baroness Wootton of Abinger

1964 Law and Lawyers in the United States
by Dean Erwin N. Griswold

1965 New Law for a New World?
by the Rt. Hon. Lord Tangley

1966 Other People's Law
by the Rt. Hon. Lord Kilbrandon

1967 The Contribution of English Law to South Africa Law;
and the Rule of Law in South Africa
by the Rt. Hon. O.D. Schreiner

1968 Justice in the Welfare State
by Professor H. Street

1969 The British Tradition in Canadian Law
by the Hon. Bora Laskin

1970 The English Judge
by Henry Cecil

1971 Punishment, Prison and the Public
by Professor Sir Rupert Cross

1972 Labour and the Law
by Professor Sir Otto Kahn-Freund

1973 Maladministration and its Remedies
by Sir Kenneth Wheare

1974 English Law — The New Dimension
by the Rt. Hon. Lord Scarman

1975 The Land and the Development; or, The Turmoil and
the Torment
by Sir Desmond Heap

1976 The National Insurance Commissioners
by Sir Robert Micklewait

1977 The European Communities and the Rule of Law
by Lord Mackenzie Stuart

1978 Liberty, Law and Justice
by Professor Sir Norman Anderson

1979 Social History and Law Reform
by Professor Lord McGregor of Durris

1980 Constitutional Fundamentals
by Professor Sir William Wade

1981 Intolerable Inquisition? Reflections on the Law of Tax
by Hubert Monroe

1982 The Quest for Security: Employees, Tenants, Wives
by Professor Tony Honore

1983 Hamlyn Revisited: The British Legal System Today
by Lord Hailsham of St. Marylebone.

1984 The Development of Consumer Law and Policy — Bold
Spirits and Timorous Souls
by Sir Gordon Borrie

1985 Law and Order
by Professor Ralf Dahrendorf

1986 The Fabric of English Civil Justice
by Sir Jack Jacob

1987 Pragmatism and Theory in English Law
by P.S. Atiyah

1988 Justification and Excuse in the Criminal Law
by J.C. Smith

1989 Protection of the Public — A New Challenge
by the Rt. Hon. Lord Justice Woolf

1990 The United Kingdom and Human Rights
by Dr. Claire Palley

1991 Introducing A European Legal Order
by Gordon Slynn

THE HAMLYN TRUST

The Hamlyn Trust came into existence under the will of the late Miss Emma Warburton Hamlyn, of Torquay, who died in 1941 at the age of eighty. She came of an old and well-known Devon Family. Her father, William Bussell Hamlyn, practised in Torquay as a solicitor for many years. She was a woman of strong character, intelligent and cultured, well-versed in literature, music and art, and a lover of her country. She inherited an interest in law. She also travelled frequently to the Continent and about the Mediterranean, and gathered impressions of comparitive jurisprudence and ethnology.

Miss Hamlyn bequeathed the residue of her estate in terms which were thought vague. The matter was taken to the Chancery Division of the High Court, which on November 29, 1948, approved a Scheme for the administration of the Trust. Paragraph 3 of the Scheme is as follows:

"The object of the charity is the furtherance by lectures or otherwise among the Common People of the United Kingdom of Great Britain and Northern Ireland of the knowledge of the Comparative Jurisprudence and Ethnology of the Chief European countries including the United Kingdom, and the circumstances of the growth of such jurisprudence to the intent that the Common People of the United Kingdom may realise the privileges which in law and custom they enjoy in comparison with other European Peoples and realising and appreciating such privileges may recognise the responsibilities and obligations attaching to them."

The Trustees are to include the Vice-Chancellor of the University of Exeter, representatives of the Universities of

xi

London, Leeds, Glasgow, Belfast and Wales and persons co-opted.

The Trustees under the scheme number nine:

Professor J.A. Andrews, M.A., B.C.L.
The Rt.-Hon. Lord Justice Butler-Sloss, D.B.E.
Professor T.C. Daintith, M.A.
Professor D.S. Greer, B.C.L., LL.B.
D Harrison, M.A.Ph.D., Sc.D., F.R.S.C., F.I.Chem.E.
Professor B. Hogan, LL.B.
Professor A.I. Ogus, M.A., B.C.L.
Professor D.M. Walker, C.B.E., Q.C., M.A., Ph.D., LL.D., F.B.A., F.R.S.E. (Chairman)
Professor Dorothy E.C. Wedderburn, M.A., D.Litt.

From the first the Trustees decided to organise courses of lectures of outstanding interest and quality by persons of eminence, under the auspices of co-operating Universities or other bodies, with a view to the lectures being made available in book form to a wide public.

The forty-third series of Hamlyn Lectures was delivered at the University of Birmingham in November—December 1991.

December 1991

DAVID M. WALKER
Chairman of the Trustees

PREFACE

One of the new experiences for an English judge going to the European Court is the collaboration of "référendaires," whom the United States judge would call "law clerks." I have been singularly fortunate in having Jacqueline Minor, Jean-Yves de Cara and Michael Wilderspin as my référendaires. They know so much and are so encouraging. I am very grateful for their help and advice in preparing these lectures, as I am for the dedicated assistance of Victoria Carter, who took charge of the "production" side and whose skill in finding materials and making the illegible comprehensible is legendary amongst my référendaires over the years. She and John Hambly have also done sterling work on what, for some reason, is called a word processor.

I was particularly pleased to have been invited by the Dean, Professor Ian Scott, to give these lectures in the Law Faculty of the University of Birmingham, one of the first English universities to introduce European Community law under the leadership of Professor Neville Brown OBE, and in the year of the foundation of its Institute of European Law, with Dr. Julian Lonbay as Director.

INTRODUCTION

"Un jour viendra où vous France, vous Russie, vous Italie, vous Angleterre, vous Allemagne, vous toutes nations du continent, sans perdre vos qualités distinctes et votre glorieuse individualité, vous vous fondrez étroitement dans une unité supérieure, et vous constituerez la fraternité européenne ... Un jour viendra où il n'y aura plus d'autres champs de bataille que les marchés s'ouvrant au commerce et les esprits s'ouvrant aux idées." (Victor Hugo, 1802–1885)

The idea of European unity obviously is not new. In the light of contemporary discussions as to the states of Central Europe associating with or joining the Community, it is interesting to recall the proposals of the fifteenth century king of Bohemia, George Podiebrady. These recognised, already at that time, the need for a supranational mechanism including, for example, majority voting amongst states and a court of justice. Even earlier, Pierre Dubois, the contemporary of Philippe le Bel, King of France, had visualised a system of institutionalised arbitration in the interests of preserving the peace.

In practice, however, attempts to achieve European unity have been largely by force from the Romans to Charlemagne to Napoleon.

By the twentieth century, some of the factors favouring the integration of Europe, which existed earlier, had disappeared. The concept of universal monarchy exemplified by the Holy Roman Empire had been replaced by that of the nation-state, which was by the nineteenth century and, in many people's eyes, is still today the paradigm of government. Latin had gone as the common language of institutions and the universities, replaced by the growth of cultural diversity in vernacular tongues. Orthodox and Protestant faiths had long since split from the Catholic Church. In addition, the influence began to be felt, particularly in ex-colonial powers, of diverse non-European cultural influences.

Nonetheless, there were those who, before the Second World War, urged some form of European union. They may have been right but their ideas were politically premature.

The devastation caused by the war, the need to rebuild, psychologically, physically and economically, gave a different opportunity which could well have been missed. Instead, the founding fathers of the new Europe (interestingly enough largely men from frontier regions which are well used to conflict of all kinds) with a rare combination of vision and realism, saw the need to avoid future conflict between Germany and France, to provide a system whereby the economies of the States could be revived on a co-operative rather than on an individual basis. Only in such a way could Europe compete in world trade, feed its peoples through a common agricultural policy and, perhaps not least, establish a bulwark against Soviet expansionism.

After an experiment with the coal and steel industries, an experiment which showed that "supranational" control could work, the founding fathers moved on to deal with the economy as a whole in the Treaty of Rome of 1957.

Lawyers often remind us at the Court of the definition in the Treaty of Rome of the "activities of the Community" for the purposes of the Community's "task" as an aid to construing other more specific articles of the Treaty. They are right to do so since those activities give an overall picture of what was and is to be done even if they do not confer enforceable rights in themselves. It is no less relevant, on an occasion such as this, to go further back—to remind oneself of the Preamble to the Treaty signed on behalf of the Sovereigns and the Presidents of the six Member States which initially formed the Community. Each recital merits reflection. The States were first "determined to lay the foundations of an ever closer union among the peoples of Europe." They resolved to ensure economic and social progress by removing the barriers which divided Europe. They affirmed as "the essential objective of their efforts the constant improvement of the living and working conditions of their peoples," and they wished to remove restrictions on internal and international trade. They were anxious to reduce the differences existing between the various regions and the backwardness of the less favoured regions. Finally, they "Resolved by thus pooling their resources to preserve and strengthen peace and liberty, and calling upon the other peoples of Europe who share their ideal to join in their efforts."

These aims are very broad and the emphasis is on economic factors—as is to be expected. The founding fathers did not, however, conceal the fact that their long-term goal was a political union. Economic convergence through the setting up of the common market was a means to that end. As Jean Monnet stated, when taking up his functions as President of the High Authority, "Europe cannot be limited to coal and steel ... the Community institution, which is the skeleton of a federal state, only makes sense if it leads to true political authority."

This view is clearly not today shared by everyone. Protagonists of the "Europe of the nation states" see the Community as a common market giving, no doubt, considerable economic benefits, but one which must not weaken national sovereignty, national independence and national identity. To them the initiative must remain with the Member States, the supranational institutions being limited as far as possible.

On the other hand, those who seek increased integration see economic convergence and increased interdependence, accentuated by the creation of the single market, as leading logically, if not inexorably, towards a greater degree of union, even political union. They rightly point out that some degree of sovereignty was expressly and inevitably surrendered by those who launched the Community and those who acceded to it—the administration of customs duties in relation to third countries and rights and obligations under the GATT, to mention obvious examples. They see the process itself, not in terms of surrendering sovereignty but of pooling sovereignty in certain areas for the good of all.

1. ESTABLISHING A COURT

At the time of our entry into the European Economic Community, many people thought that the vast majority of men and women in this country would never directly feel the impact of Community law.

Miss Hamlyn's intention was that these lectures which bear her name should be of relevance to the man and woman in the street rather than that they should lay the foundations for a Hart-Devlin type discussion between a small group of specialist professors. In view of the attitude to which I have referred, it may, therefore, be asked whether it is appropriate that one of this series of lectures should be devoted to a consideration of European Community law and practice.

The Trustees feel that it is. "1992" is approaching. As a date it has become a symbol and a challenge. It has provoked among people in the street more interest in the Community than ever before. As an imminent event it seems to have led manufacturers, traders and the professions not only to appreciate the opportunities which participation in the Community gives them but to want actively and successfully to benefit from those opportunities. It has induced lawyers and businessmen throughout the rest of the English-speaking world (and I suppose elsewhere) to look closely at what is being done in the Community. Universities in the English-speaking world increasingly teach and study Community law, particularly the jurisprudence of the Court.

The Community, at the same time, is an object of great interest to other areas where regionalism is on the move—the Andean Pact, Asia, the Pacific, to mention only a few—and the participation of the United Kingdom inevitably attracts the particular attention of those who share the common law and our common language. The United States-Canada free trade agreement, their negotiations with Mexico and current discussions concerning a grouping of the southern states of South America, have provided further, if less direct, reasons for interest in what is going on in the Community.

On the other hand, there are doubts and fears which cannot be ignored. Our trading partners worry about a "fortress Europe" which may result from "an area without internal frontiers." There is anxiety here (though I do not think we should assume that the anxiety is exclusive to the United Kingdom) that too much is being surrendered. "No loss of sovereignty," "No federation" have become battle cries reflecting fears which may have been felt not only today but at other times when states have bonded together in their common interest.

It is for the politicians to deal with these doubts and fears, for governments and parliaments to decide how far we are to go, in what direction and at what speed. The Maastricht conference, now only days away, will be of great importance. What governments and parliaments decide will govern the content of future treaties between the Member States and the content of subordinate Community legislation.

Throughout the history of the Community, however, the Court of Justice has had a remarkable role to pay—as Jeremy Lever Q.C. said to us in one case, the Court's jurisprudence is "the cement which holds the structure together."

It seemed to me appropriate therefore, as we approach 1992, to take stock of the Court's position. The British seem to have an innate interest in the workings of their courts and the administration of justice which is not just derived from the triumphs of Rumpole. Since the Court of Justice is now an integral part of the administration, if not of English law at least of the law applicable in England, it is important that its role should be understood. People are not helped to such an understanding by the frequent confusion in the media—and in the speeches of politicians—between the European Court of Justice, which sits in Luxembourg, the European Court of Human Rights, which is not an institution of the European Community and which sits in Strasbourg, and the International Court of Justice, which sits in The Hague. My aim, in the light of the objectives of the Trust, is to show something of what we are and what we do in Luxembourg.

To review the full ambit of the Court's jurisprudence would obviously be impossible even in 10 lectures, assuming that anyone in the audience had the stamina to survive for so long. The enquiry must be more limited and necessarily selective. My plan is, therefore, to look in these four lectures at the function of the Court, making some comparisons in the context of the EEC Treaty with what seem to be comparable courts; then to illustrate the effect of the Court's decisions in the United Kingdom, first on commerce and then on the lives of people; finally, and perhaps more debatably, to consider whether the Court's practices and procedures are appropriate to its current and its expanding task.

I should perhaps declare an interest which may become evident. When I was asked to go to the European Court by Lord Hailsham, I made it clear that if I went I should go as a technician and not as a missionary for any particular European ideal. We were part of the Community and there was a job to be done. I am now no less clear that "Europe" cannot go backwards or stand still however slowly it moves forward (and speed is not in my view a prerequisite of success in many areas of Community development or in the growth of the Court's jurisprudence). I am also convinced that the United Kingdom and the common law have a significant contribution to make and that we only stand any chance of achieving the sort of Community that we really want if we actively and positively make that contribution not only on the political but also on the cultural and the legal level.

There is, as I see it, in the United Kingdom anxiety about losing not only sovereignty but also our national culture and identity. This is a natural reaction but I do not see it as an object or as a result of the sort of Community which is at present being built. Independent national cultures are not in conflict with the Community aim. They are complementary to it and it is only by them that the Community system can be enriched.

The courtroom at Luxembourg is in some ways a microcosm of what is happening outside. The lawyers who come to argue the cases wear their national robes—the English, Scottish and Irish in their wigs, the Italians with their gold and silver tassels, the Germans with their elegant silk facings and white ties, the Dutch with their long many-buttoned black gowns, the French with the ermine band to the "épinonge" they wear over their shoulder. They address the Court according to their national customs. So the English begin "My Lords," some of the others "Monsieur le Président, Messieurs les Juges, Monsieur l'Avocat général" or "Herr Präsident, meine Herren Richter, mein Herr Generalanwalt." They reveal their national characteristics in the manner of their address. In answer to a question from the Court, the staccato Scottish "certainly" is very different from the rolling Italian "assolutamente," pregnant with emphasis and followed by an exuberant explanation. Even to compare the hands of the interpreters in the Dutch and the Danish booths with those in the Italian and French booths—as many visiting students do to their apparent interest—is significant. The witticisms of the advocates, if infrequent, are very different in character; the literary quotations, national in origin. And there is pride in it. I well remember a vigorous discussion during a hearing between the Irish judge, Justice O'Higgins, and myself as to whether a couplet which I had quoted to counsel came from the Englishman, Pope, or, as he insisted, from the Irishman, Goldsmith.

The legal systems and experiences which the lawyers draw on are patently so different, both in the substance of their submissions and in their techniques. A stranger would quickly realise which lawyers come from a country where oral advocacy and debate between the judge and the lawyer is the norm. Even, dare I say it, when one of the 13 judges and the six advocates general speak from the bench, whether in their own language or in French, a lot of national history and tradition and personality is evident which is not hidden behind the identical red gowns which they all wear.

No one would want to change any of this; and yet they are all met together to produce a European legal system, the law of a region, appropriate to a common market, and to achieve the objectives of the Treaty through a court which, in a limited area, is the Supreme

Court of Europe. This Court is the crucible in which legal principles and developments are to be fused.

What kind of court?

When the Community was founded it was obvious that there would be disputes between the Member States, between them and the institutions of the Community (the Council and the Commission and the Parliament), between the institutions themselves. It was equally obvious that issues would arise which concerned individuals, persons and limited companies, in a Community law context. Some form of adjudication was necessary, indeed inevitable.

It might have been possible to have followed the example of the United States of America, and to have created a Community network of "federal" courts with a supreme court atop the hierarchy.

The decision by the draftsmen of the United States Constitution to permit Congress to create a national network of federal courts[1] seems to have been due to a fear that state courts would be too deferential to "local spirit," especially since state judges did not enjoy security of tenure.[2] I do not think that the converse was a reason for not adopting the federal system in the Community. I suspect that it was not done partly because it was not considered that the volume of cases was likely to justify, even on the basis of cost, a complete federal system of courts.

Moreover, even if political union was the ultimate goal, there was no blueprint for a federation in any

---

[1] See Article I, s.8 and Article III of the United States Constitution.
[2] See *The Federalist*, No. 81 (Alexander Hamilton).

sense comparable with that of the United States. True, the United States Constitution refers to the creation of "a more perfect Union" and the Treaty of Rome speaks of "an ever closer union amongst the peoples of Europe"; true, also, the states were distinct and preserved their identities and laws in many ways—even in the nineteenth century, the speeches of Jefferson Davis before the Civil War emphasising state rights are paralleled by much that has been said by politicians in recent years inside Europe and, perhaps particularly, in the United Kingdom. Yet, there were many differences between the United States and the European Economic Community both in their conception and in their realisation.

There were differences too between the European Community and the other two great English-speaking federations of what has been called an "integrative"[3] as opposed to a "devolutionary"[4] type, namely Australia and Canada. Thus, for example, the three federations came into being as a result of their gaining independence from a colonial power; the choice of a federal form of government and a judicial system was influenced by the pattern of former colonial government which had created smaller units within the territory as a whole; there was greater legal and cultural homogeneity in the grouping (I do not forget Quebec and Louisiana) since the interpretation and application of the three constitutions was

---

[3] As defined by Lenaerts in Constitutionalism and the Many Faces of Federalism (1990) 38 Am.J. of Comp.L. 205.

[4] A comparison with the Federal Republic of Germany would be relevant in a different way. Thus, Article 30 of the German Basic Law presumes that power is in the Länder and states, that the federation or Bund only has powers if they are granted specifically. By Article 72, in areas of concurrent power, the Länder are competent to act until such time as the Bund uses its legislative power and the conditions upon which the Bund's legislative powers can be set in motion are identified. Federalism in this sense works to preserve or protect the powers of the constituents rather than the federation.

largely in the hands of lawyers trained in the common law and indeed the constitutions of Canada and Australia were drafted as acts of the United Kingdom Parliament.

The exercise of those powers which are the most obvious expressions of statehood—foreign affairs, defence, taxation, coinage and monetary policy—devolved in the three federations on the central government, unlike the Community where such powers remained and, at present still remain, with the Member States. Individual citizens to a much greater extent wanted the federation and saw themselves first as citizens of the federation. The European Community was the creation of far-seeing political leaders rather than a spontaneous expression of the will of the people, who continued and continue to see themselves first as citizens of a particular Member State. Unlike the three federations, the only democratically elected institution of the Community was the one which had the least influence on legislation and the most powerful of the institutions was essentially representative of the Member States.

In a word, politically, a parallel federal structure of courts was premature. It does not follow that such a structure might not one day have to be considered as the scope of Community law is extended.

Another possibility, at the beginning, might have been to vest all jurisdiction over Community law matters in national courts with a right of appeal to one central court or to regional courts of appeal. One apparent argument against such a structure is that some matters ought to go direct to a central Community court—those involving constitutional issues or relations between States. Since, in addition, it could be assumed that only a small percentage of cases involving Community law issues would go on appeal, the diversity of courts was likely to lead to considerable diversity of decision-making. I doubt in any event, whether politically the notion of a direct "appeal" from a Member State's supreme court to a central court would have been acceptable.

Instead of either of these a system was adopted which divided cases into two types with separate procedures. In the first type of procedure disputes between States and institutions or between individuals and institutions go direct to the Court which, until the Court of First Instance was created, was the court of first, last and only resort since the Member States had undertaken to settle their disputes only in accordance with the provisions of the Treaty. These are truly "federal" questions and in the United States, Canada and Australia would go to the federal court—in this respect a comparison with the Australian Constitution seems to be particularly relevant.

The second type of case—largely disputes between individuals or between individuals and Member States or agencies of the Member States carrying out Community administration—follows a procedure different from that adopted for the first type of case. In this second type of case, the three federal systems provide for an appeal. The Treaty of Rome created a unique system whereby national courts, before which a question of interpretation of the Treaty or the interpretation or validity of subordinate legislation arose, could, or in certain cases must, refer a question to the Court of Justice.

This procedure has created a remarkable relationship of comity between national courts and the Court of Justice. In one sense, Article 177, which creates the procedure, can be seen as a specific expression of the duties of mutual co-operation and assistance imposed upon the Governments and institutions by Article 5 of the Treaty. Indeed, the Court has recently confirmed that Article 5 of the Treaty applies to co-operation between the Community and the judicial authorities of the Member States as well as to legislative and executive bodies.[5] It is a procedure which has worked extraordinarily well, giving rise to declaratory judgments which have laid down some of the most important general principles of Community law as well as those which have interpreted in detail Community legislation.

The Court, often to the surprise of American lawyers, has no power to "call in" questions of Community law arising in litigation before the national judge and the parties have no right to insist on a reference so that some important questions may not reach the Court. On the other hand, persistent refusal by national courts of last resort to refer questions would amount to a breach of the Treaty, though it is unlikely that the Commission would apply to the Court for a declaration that a Member State was in breach of its obligation except in an extreme case. In such a case it seems likely that the Member State would have shown in other ways its intention to disregard Community law.

Conversely, there is no procedure by which the Court can select from the questions put to it those which it chooses to answer, and reject the rest, as does in effect the Supreme Court of the United States by the process of certiorari.

Yet, overall, I have the impression that the important questions do come, even if it takes years before they reach the Court, and I do not have any general feeling of national courts running amok on Community law issues.

Some of the national "supreme" courts may have disapproved of the Court's decisions from time to time as, for example, in relation to the enforcement of directives which have not been implemented in national legislation or those which concern the relationship of

---

[5] Case C–2/88 Imm. *Zwartfeld*, Order of July 13, 1990 [1990] E.C.R. I–3365.

national fundamental laws and Community law. Yet I have never been conscious of resentment that questions can be or have to be referred to a court only one of the members of which is of the same nationality as the referring court.

I do not think that the relationship which exists can be put better than by citing a passage from the judgment of Mr. Justice Bingham when considering whether to exercise his discretion to make a request for a preliminary ruling in *Commissioner of Customs and Excise* v. *Aps Samex*.[6] Mr. Justice Bingham said:

"as a judge in a national court, asked to decide questions of Community law, I am very conscious of the advantages enjoyed by the Court of Justice. It has a panoramic view of the Community and its institutions, a detailed knowledge of the treaties and of much subordinate legislation made under them, and an intimate familiarity with the functioning of the Community Market which no national judge denied the collective experience of the Court of Justice could hope to achieve. Where questions of administrative intention and practice arise the Court of Justice can receive submissions from the Community institutions, as also where relations between the Community and non-member states are in issue. Where the interests of member states are affected they can intervene to make their views known. That is a material consideration in this case since there is some slight evidence that the practice of different member states is divergent. Where comparison falls to be made between Community texts in different languages, all texts being equally authentic, the multinational Court of Justice is equipped to

---

[6] [1983] 1 All E.R. 1042; [1983] 3 C.M.L.R. 194. The reference to the European Court (Case 34/83) was later withdrawn.

carry out the task in a way which no national judge, whatever his linguistic skills, could rival. The interpretation of Community instruments involves very often not the process familiar to common lawyers of laboriously extracting the meaning from words used but the more creative process of supplying flesh to a spare and loosely constructed skeleton. The choice between alternative submissions may turn not on purely legal considerations, but on a broader view of what the orderly development of the Community requires. These are matters which the Court of Justice is very much better placed to assess and determine than a national court.''

The speech of Lord Templeman in *Foster* v. *British Gas*,[7] applying the answer given by the Court to an important question referred by the House of Lords,[8] shows in the fullest sense how the ''dialogue'' between the courts is completed and made effective.

The Court has rarely refused a question unless it finds it to be outside the scope of the reference procedure. It has gone to great lengths to avoid taking over the function of the national judge in actually deciding the case before him or in ruling on the validity or interpretation of national laws. Conversely, the Court has reserved to itself the power to declare acts of the Community institutions to be invalid on the ground that conflicting national decisions on validity would place in jeopardy the very unity of the Community legal order and detract from the fundamental requirement of legal certainty. Thus any national court or tribunal which concludes that the outcome of a case pending before it turned on the validity or otherwise of a Community law

[7] [1991] 2 All E.R. 705.
[8] Case 188/89 [1990] E.C.R. 3343.

measure *and* considers that there are serious doubts as to its validity, must make a reference to Luxembourg in this respect.[9] The Court has created for itself a position similar to that which exists in some national legal orders where the power to declare legislation unconstitutional, and thus invalid, is confined to a specialised constitutional court.[10]

How can the system be made effective?

This avenue of jurisdiction has not only led to the establishment of important principles of law, it has made it possible for there to be uniformity in the administration of Community law by national courts. If there were no central court which could give definitive rulings on the validity of Community subordinate legislation or as to its interpretation then divergence between different national courts would be inevitable. It may even seem surprising that there should have been arguments as to whether the Court's ruling as to validity or interpretation in one case (which was clearly binding on all courts dealing with the case in question) should also be binding on judges dealing with other cases where the same issue arose. The ruling is now accepted as applying generally on validity and on interpretation; the judge in another case can always refer the question back to the Court.[11]

In a union of states, however, uniformity is not the only essential feature if the law of the union and the

---

[9] Case 314/85 *Foto-Frost* v. *Hauptzollamt Lübeck-Ost* [1987] E.C.R. 4199.

[10] See, for example, the situation in Italy. The exclusive jurisdiction of the Corte Costituzionale applies only where Italian legislation is said to be contrary to the Italian Constitution. Where the legislation contravenes Community law, any Italian court may declare it invalid (Case 35/76 *Simmenthal* [1976] E.C.R. 1871).

[11] See Joined Cases 28–30/62 *Da Costa* [1963] E.C.R. 61.

court of the union is to coexist with national law and national courts. In the first place, it has to be decided whether the law of the union prevails over national law if there is a conflict, and, in the second place, if it is to prevail, there must be a central court which is competent to create and maintain a hierarchy of norms and which can define and enforce areas of competence—in effect, judicial review on the constitutional level.

It is of interest to compare the experience of the Community with that of the three federations which I have mentioned.

In the United States Constitution the position is clear. By Article VI, cl. 2:

> "This Constitution and the laws of the United States which shall be made in pursuance thereof ... shall be the supreme law of the land, and the judges in every state shall be bound thereby, any thing in the constitution or laws of any state to the contrary notwithstanding."

It was on this Article that the famous judgment of Chief Justice Marshall in *Marbury* v. *Madison*[12] was based and which showed that acts of Congress not in accordance with the Constitution could be struck down. So equally was the decision in *Martin* v. *Hunter's Lessee*,[13] where Justice Story emphasised the Supreme Court's right and duty to be the single, final interpreter of the Constitution. Moreover, the Court said there had to be a uniform interpretation throughout the nation. To the argument that the states remained sovereign the Justice replied that the people of the nation had chosen to limit state

[12] 5 U.S. (1 Cranch) 137 at 180 (1803).
[13] 14 U.S. (1 Wheat) 304 (1816).

sovereignty when they established a constitution specifically restricting state acts in a variety of ways—a reply which we need to remind ourselves of at times of political conflict.

The Australian Constitution has a comparable provision in section 109—"when a law is inconsistent with the law of the Commonwealth, the latter shall prevail and the former shall, to the extent of the inconsistency, be invalid." In Canada, the 1867 Constitution Act implicitly recognised the dominance of federal law in section 90 but the position was, for the first time, made explicit in section 52(1) of the 1982 Constitution Act—"The Constitution is the supreme law of Canada and any law that is inconsistent with the provisions of the Constitution is to the extent of the inconsistency of no force and effect."

Unlike the constitutions of the United States, Canada and Australia, the Treaty of Rome contains no "supremacy clause." Supremacy, in Community law, is the creation of the judges. In *Costa* v. *ENEL*,[14] the Court, in language strongly reminiscent of Justice Story's in *Martin* v. *Hunter's Lessee* ruled that "by creating a Community of unlimited duration, having its own institutions, its own personality ... and ... real powers stemming from a limitation or a transfer of powers from the States to the Community, the Member States have limited their sovereign rights ... and have thus created a body of law which binds both their nationals and themselves."

It is in dealing with the relationship between Community law and national law that the Court's judgments have been so far-reaching. Even two years before *Costa* v. *ENEL*, the Court had recognised that the Community had created a new legal order which not only bound the Member States but which imposed obligations and conferred rights on citizens, the latter of which they

[14] Case 6/64 [1964] E.C.R. 1143.

could enforce directly in the national courts.[15] Where provisions of the Treaty were sufficiently clear and unconditional, the citizen could rely on them in the national court without their having to be incorporated into national legislation. To apply this rule to regulations, which are binding in their entirety and directly applicable in all Member States, was not a great further step. The position as to directives, which are only binding on the Member States to whom they are addressed and as to the result to be achieved and which leave to the Member States the choice of form and methods, was very different. Nonetheless, the Court has recognised that, if national legislation cannot be construed as being compatible with a directive which has not been adopted, the citizen may be able to rely in the national courts as against the Member State on the provisions of a directive which are sufficiently clear and unconditional, where the Member State has failed to implement the directive properly or at all.[16]

Erecting the twin pillars of direct effect and supremacy, including supremacy over subsequently adopted national legislation which is incompatible with Community law, may have been revolutionary at the time. They are now regarded as essential. They come together in the rule that national courts must make Community law effective, even overriding national law[17] and national procedural rules which would otherwise impede an effective remedy under Community law. From this flowed inexorably the decision in *Factortame*.[18] The English rule that no interim injunction could be granted

---

[15] Case 26/62 *Van Gend en Loos* [1963] E.C.R. 3.
[16] Case 152/84 *Marshall* v. *Southampton and South West Hampshire Area Health Authority* [1986] E.C.R. 723.
[17] Case 106/77 *Simmenthal* [1978] E.C.R. 629.
[18] Case C–213/89 *Factortame* v. *Secretary of State for Transport* [1990] E.C.R. I–2433.

against the Crown could not be relied on to prevent a judge from granting interim relief which he would have granted under Community law but for such a rule. The English judge was required to ignore that rule if he thought that an injunction was needed to make Community law rights effective. In the same vein, the Court has held that administrative authorities must obey the same rules as the national courts and give full effect to Community law.[19]

Of even greater importance than *Factortame* is the very recent decision of the Court in *Francovich and Bonifaci* v. *Italy*.[20] The case concerned an action brought against the Italian State by two workers who were heavily out of pocket when their employer became insolvent owing them arrears of salary. The Italian Government had not transposed a directive which, *inter alia*, provides for the creation of guarantee funds to secure the salaries of employed persons in the event of the insolvency of their employer.[21] The Court held that this directive was not sufficiently precise and unconditional to be directly effective. Accepting that Community rights would not be effective if individuals could not be compensated when such rights were violated by a Member State, the Member State was obliged to provide redress to individuals prejudiced by the failure to transpose the directive. Following this judgment, individuals will be able to claim damages against a Member State if they have suffered harm as a direct result of that State's failure to transpose a directive provided that the directive is for the benefit of individuals, that the content of the rights granted to individuals can be identified

[19] Case 103/88 *Costanzo* [1989] E.C.R. 1839.
[20] Joined Cases 6 and 9/90, judgment of November 19, 1991, not yet reported.
[21] Council Directive 80/987/EEC, O.J.L. 283, p. 23.

from the provisions of the directive, and that there is a causal link between the harm suffered and the breach of the Member State's obligation to transpose.

The decision is a logical step in the line of direct effect/supremacy of Community law cases. As the Advocate-General pointed out in his Opinion, the question of whether a directive is directly effective or not is merely a technical matter turning on whether its provisions are sufficiently precise and unconditional. If that criterion were not satisfied in a given case, the effectiveness of Community law would be compromised if a Member State were able to rely on its own wrongdoing in not transposing the directive in order to evade obligations flowing from it. Following the ruling in *Francovich and Bonifaci*, provisions in an unimplemented directive can be invoked either directly against the Member State via the doctrine of direct effectiveness or indirectly via the obligation to provide redress for the harm suffered from the failure to transpose.

The Court's elaboration of the theory of primacy of Community law sprang, perhaps, from the coming together of many influences—the example of the United States Supreme Court, the traditionally "monist" approach of most of the original Member States to the incorporation of international law, and the compelling need to endow the new legal order with "effet utile." In the absence of a hierarchy of norms, the uniform interpretation of Community law would be imperilled. Although Article 177 enables the European Court to provide definitive rulings on the interpretation of the Treaty and of Community legislation, these rulings would be of little value if the effect of Community measures could be undermined by national court decisions or by the simple enactment of conflicting national legislation. It is the appreciation of this which underlies the general willingness of national courts to accept and apply the doctrine of supremacy. Failure to accord supremacy to Community law would, in a very short time, have led to a breakdown of the "new legal order."

Only the French Conseil d'Etat, in the period between its judgments in the *Semoules* case[22] and the *Nicolo* case,[23] refused to accept that in the event of a conflict between Community law and subsequent national legislation, the former must prevail.

Following the *Factortame*[24] decision it was often overlooked by irate commentators that the doctrine of the supremacy of Community law was not, in itself, called into question. As Lord Bridge put it:

"If the supremacy within the European Community of Community law was not always inherent in the EEC Treaty, it was certainly well-established in the jurisprudence of the Court of Justice long before the United Kingdom joined the Community. Thus, whatever limitation of its sovereignty Parliament accepted when it enacted the European Communities Act 1972 was entirely voluntary under the terms of the Act of 1972. It has always been clear that it was the duty of a United Kingdom court, when delivering final judgment, to override any rule of national law found to be in conflict with any directly enforceable rule of Community law."

Whilst a purist might argue that the duty of English courts to disapply conflicting national rules of law flows

---

[22] *Syndicat général des fabricants de semoules de France* [1970] C.M.L.R. 395.
[23] Conseil d'Etat, judgment of October 20, 1989, noted by David Pollard in European Law Review (June 1990), Vol. 15, No. 3, p. 267.
[24] Case C–213/89, *supra*.

directly from the Treaty, and not from the European
Communities Act, Lord Bridge's observations, which
were plainly right but from which others shrink, display
an unqualified acceptance of a fundamental limitation to
the doctrine of sovereignty of Parliament.

Nor is compliance with the rule of primacy confined to
the judicial branch of government. Throughout the
Factortame litigation, the British Government accepted
that if the Merchant Shipping Act 1988 was found to
conflict with any of the provisions of the Treaty it would
stand in need of amendment. Indeed, following the
Order of the President of the European Court in Case
246/89R[25] (the direct action brought by the Commission
against the United Kingdom), that the requirement that
the owner, operator or charterer of a fishing boat be a
British national was contrary to Articles 7 and 52 of the
Treaty, the Government moved very quickly to abrogate
the relevant provision of the Merchant Shipping Act.[26]

Similarly, in a number of sex discrimination and social
security cases, the British Government has acted with
remarkable rapidity to give effect to Community law, in
one case even acting between the Opinion of the
Advocate-General and the judgment of the Court.[27]

And so, in relation to supremacy, we have achieved in
the Community by judicial decision what is contained in
the Constitutions of the three federations.

As to the second point—the power of judicial
review—there is no explicit grant of the power of judicial
review in the United States Constitution nor in the

---

[25] *Commission* v. *United Kingdom* [1989] E.C.R. 3125.

[26] By the Merchant Shipping Act 1988 (Amendment) Order 1989. See,
now, judgment of July 25, 1991 in Case C–221/89 *Factortame* v.
Secretary of State for Transport and in Case C–246/89 *Commission* v.
United Kingdom, judgment of October 4, 1991, not yet reported.

[27] Case 150/85 *Drake* v. *Chief Adjudication Officer* [1986] E.C.R. 1995.

Australian and Canadian Constitutions. The power of judicial review was established by the United States Supreme Court in 1803 in *Marbury* v. *Madison*.[28] It is implicit in section 74 of the Australian Constitution that the High Court has such power, which it has certainly exercised. The Canadian position is rather more curious since the British North America Act 1867, as an imperial statute, had overriding force by virtue of the Colonial Laws Validity Act 1865, s.2, which provided that any Colonial law which was repugnant to an imperial statute "extending to the colony" was void to the extent of the repugnancy. The doctrine of judicial review of federal and provincial legislation in Canada is, therefore, somewhat ironically, a consequence of the theory of the sovereignty of the (then) imperial Parliament.[29]

Since 1982 with the Constitution Act and the Charter of Rights and Freedoms, the Supreme Court has stated, in *Law Society of Upper Canada* v. *Skapinker*,[30] that "with the Constitution Act 1982 comes a new dimension . . . a dimension which like the balance of the Constitution, remains to be interpreted and applied by the Court."

In the Community the position is again the converse since there is a specific power in Article 173 of the EEC Treaty "to review the legality of acts of the Council and the Commission," and the power in Article 177 to give preliminary rulings concerning, *inter alia*, the validity of acts of the institutions of the Community.

Where the Court finds that an act of the institutions infringes the Treaty or amounts to a misuse of powers, the Court declares it void and the institutions must take

---

[28] *Supra.*

[29] See generally Strayer, *The Canadian Constitution and the Courts* (Toronto, 1988) and Hogg, *Constitutional Law of Canada* (Toronto, 1977).

[30] [1984] 1 S.C.R. 357.

the "necessary measures to comply with the judgment of the Court."

Control by the Court of national measures is less direct but nonetheless effective in practice. If the Commission considers that a Member State is in breach of the Treaty (as for example by maintaining legislation which is in conflict with it) then the Court can be asked to make a declaration to that effect under Article 169 of the Treaty. If it does so, the State must "take the necessary measures to comply with" the Court's judgment. This, in effect, involves changing the national legislation to conform with Community law or the matter may be brought back before the Court. The Court does not, however, declare void the national legislation as it does the Community act. Similarly, on an Article 177 reference, it will not give a ruling on specific national legislation. It will say no more than that a provision of the same effect as the national provision in question is in conflict with Community law. The effect, however, is not far different from that achieved in *Martin* v. *Hunter's Lessee*. As the Court explained in *Foglia* v. *Novello*,[31] "an individual whose rights are infringed by measures adopted by a Member State which are contrary to Community law must have the opportunity to seek the protection of a court possessed of jurisdiction and that such a court, for its part, must be free to obtain information as to the scope of the relevant provisions of Community law by the procedure under Article 177."

This procedure and the principles of supremacy and direct effect enable the citizen to rely on sufficiently clear and precise provisions of Community law and require the national courts to strike down measures of national law offending against it. At the same time, they respect

[31] Case 244/80 [1981] E.C.R. 3066.

the "sovereignty" of national courts in relation to national law.

The Community and the Member States

A matter of prime importance in the creation of a union is to define the competence of the parts as opposed to the composite—the states as opposed to the "federation."

The Australian Constitution lists the legislative powers of the Commonwealth in sections 51 and 52; the legislative competence of the states is preserved unless the Commonwealth exercises its power to exclude the operation of the state legislature. The Canadian Constitution Act of 1867 sets out the respective powers of the provincial legislatures and the federal parliament respectively, though section 91 reserved to the federal parliament a residual power: "To make laws for the peace, order and good government of Canada, in relation to all matters not coming within the classes of subjects by this Act assigned exclusively to the legislatures of the provinces." The United States Constitution and the Treaty of Rome enumerate the powers of the Federal government and the Community respectively; all remaining legislative competence is in the hands of the States or Member States.

The Court has, in my view, adopted a reasonably liberal but not excessively federalist approach to the interpretation of articles of the Treaty conferring powers on the institutions perhaps at the expense of the Member States. Generally, the Treaty does not specify which of the competences conferred on the Community are exclusive and it has been for the Court to resolve this. Sometimes it can be said to have recognised powers vested in the Community which are not immediately obvious but which it felt were justified in the interests of making the Community work. A definition of the powers of the Community to develop a common commercial policy by international trade agreements thereby making inroads into the treaty options of the Member States is one example.[32] The Court gradually recognised that the Community's powers must lead to the exclusion of concurrent powers exercisable by the Member States[33] other than in specific areas, as where the Community specifically authorised them to act[34] or where existing obligations necessarily had to be carried out by the Member States.

Moreover, the Court has recognised that even where the Community institutions have failed to act when powers were given to them, Member States cannot act unilaterally. They must at the least co-operate with and consult the Commission. Since the failure to act may be a deliberate choice of economic policy in an area attributed by the Member States to the Community.[35]

There is, however, another way in which the Court may become involved in deciding between the competence of the Member States and the Community. By Article 130R of the Treaty, inserted by the Single European Act, action by the Community relating to the environment shall have the objectives of preserving, protecting and improving the quality of the environment, contributing towards protecting human health and ensuring a prudent and rational utilisation of natural

[32] Case 45/86 *Commission* v. *Council* [1987] E.C.R. 1493.
[33] Opinion 1/75 [1975] E.C.R. 1355.
[34] Case 41/76 *Donckerwolcke* [1976] E.C.R. 1921, Case 174/84 *Bulk Oil* v. *Sun Oil* [1986] E.C.R. 559.
[35] Case 50/76 *Amsterdam Bulb* [1977] E.C.R. 137; Case 111/76 *Van den Hazel* [1977] E.C.R. 901.

resources. By Article 130R(4), the Community shall take action relating to the environment to the extent to which the objectives referred to in paragraph 1 can be attained "better at Community level than at the level of the individual Member States." This reflects the principle of subsidiarity which is now propounded as a rule of more general application.

This principle calls, in the first place, for a political decision and a legislative definition. The principle seems to be, in essence, that the Community should only act when action at Community level would be more effective than action by the Member States individually. It is regarded by some as a method of protecting Member States from encroachment by the Community as is done in some other existing federations where the states need protection: by others it is regarded as a way of legitimately expanding Community powers. If it is to be accepted at all it seems more likely to be the former but on either view it calls for a definition of those areas where there may be concurrent action, as in respect of the environment, and a limitation of Community action to where it would be more effective.

Whether subsidiarity, as a general principle, involves a legal judgment is also a difficult question. Should it be subject to judicial review at all—and, if so, should it be capable only of retrospective review or should a court have power to decide in advance whether the conditions of subsidiarity are satisfied? If a decision is taken unanimously by the Member States that the principle of subsidiarity is satisfied, it is difficult to visualise how far a court should have a role to intervene. If a decision is taken by a majority of Member States, then a court, at the behest of a minority state, can become embroiled in difficult political arguments. The dispute between the Canadian provinces and the federal government, when the latter asked the British Parliament to "repatriate" the

British North America Act of 1867 and the Canadian Supreme Court was asked to give its view as to whether this could properly be done without the consent of the provinces, showed the extent of the difficulties which can result for a court in such circumstances.

Despite this, it seems to me that if this principle is to be adopted there is a role, even if limited, for the Court. There may be a strong political element but, at the end of the day, the question as to whether action by the Community could be more effective, or even whether there is material on which the Council could reasonably decide that action by the Community could be more effective, is capable of judicial decision on the basis of objective criteria. It may be that this would involve the Court in an "active" "creative" role. If a court is to be involved it is in my view incontrovertible that it is the Court of Justice which should have the last word, as with every major issue of law which calls for judicial determination. There is room for only one supreme court.

It is not for the Court but for governments to decide who does what but maybe it is worthwhile to recall Lord Radcliffe's summary of what he thought Hamilton was arguing in "The Federalist":

"Make up your minds as to what you really want," he seems to say. "That is the first essential thing. If you really think it best to place this or that branch of your affairs under the authority of some larger union then give it frankly the powers it needs to make its control effective. Do not be afraid or half-hearted in what you are doing, or take back with one hand what you give with the other."[36]

[36] *The Problem of Power*, p. 63.

The Institutions *Inter Se*

Relations between the Member States and the institutions as representing the Community are not the only area of possible conflict. The respective competences of one or other of the institutions have recently been challenged more than hitherto. There have, in the last three years, been a number of cases in which the Commission has challenged the use by the Council of an article of the Treaty specifying the need for a unanimous decision. The Commission has insisted that the appropriate provisions enable decisions to be taken by a majority.[37] It may be at first sight curious to challenge a unanimous decision on the basis that it should have been taken by a majority vote. "If it could be done unanimously it could be done by a majority" would seem to be the reply and it sounds like a lawyer's technical wrangle. This is in fact not so for two reasons. In the first place, if a Commission proposal needs only a majority decision there may be a better chance of it going through unaltered than if unanimity is required when compromise may be needed and, in the process, the proposal watered down. In the second place, a number of the articles requiring a majority decision require the co-operation procedure which involves the European Parliament, often a natural ally of the Commission against the Council, conscious as the latter is, in the first place, of the attitudes of the Member States. Some of these cases can have important consequences and the arguments each way can be strong. A good example is the directive involving the treatment

---

[37] See, for example, Case 131/87 *Commission* v. *Council* [1989] E.C.R. 3764 (Scope of Article 43) and Case C–300/89 *Commission* v. *Council*, judgment of June 11, 1991, not yet reported (Scope of Articles 100A and 130S).

and disposal of titanium dioxide waste. On the face of it there were a number of provisions clearly dealing with environmental issues so that, as the Council considered, the directive was properly made under Article 130S of the Treaty. The Commission and the Parliament contended that it should have been made under Article 100A.[38] The Court concluded that the directive could not be based on both Articles since the procedures were different. The Court recalled that environmental protection was a constituent of other Community policies; that measures taken to establish the internal market should aim for a high level of environmental protection; and, that environmental considerations could affect competition. In the present case the harmonisation of national rules relating to the production of titanium dioxide in order to eliminate the distortion of competition was designed to contribute to achieving the internal market and, therefore, should have been made under Article 100A. The Council's directive was accordingly annulled.

These challenges, however, do not concern only the Council's decisions. Thus, in *Les Verts*,[39] in striking down the allocation by the Bureau of the European Parliament of funds to be used by political parties, the Court declared that "the setting up of a scheme for the reimbursement of electoral campaign expenses ... remain within the competence of the Member States." In cases involving the migration policy,[40] a decision of the Commission was struck down on the ground, *inter alia*, that its link with the "social field" referred to in Article 118 of the Treaty was "extremely tenuous."

In a number of cases Member States also have objected to the use of an article of the Treaty permitting majority

[38] Case C–300/89, *supra*.
[39] Case 294/83 [1986] E.C.R. 1339.
[40] Case 281/85 *Germany and others* v. *Commission* [1987] E.C.R. 3203.

voting.[41] This is an important protection for the Member States when legality is the real issue, even if the initial objection to a measure is "political"; a watch will have to be kept to ensure that the arguments justifying the intervention by the Court are really ones of law and proper for judicial review.

The Court has played a part in the constitutional and political structure of the Community in another and less direct way which concerns the European Parliament. It thus held at a relatively early stage that the Parliament was able to intervene in direct actions and also that it might be asked to make submissions or give information in Article 177 references. The Court also had no difficulty in holding that certain administrative procedures of the Parliament may be subject to judicial review. Decisions affecting purely policy matters and recommendations of committees, which do not amount to administrative action by the Parliament, are not, however, subject to such a review. Those which affect the rights of third parties are. In this way the Court may have an important role in ensuring that the Parliament properly observes the procedures which are prescribed.

Of much greater importance was a case in which the Court accepted that if the Council failed to carry out an obligation under the Treaty, the Parliament might, under Article 175 of the Treaty, apply to the Court for a declaration to that effect.[42] The result of this application in relation to air transport was obviously influential in producing subsequent activity on the part of the Council. The Court, however, when asked to hold that the

---

[41] See for example, Case 68/86 *United Kingdom* v. *Council* [1988] E.C.R. 857 (Scope of Article 43) and Joined Cases C–51, 90 and 94/89 *United Kingdom, France and Germany* v. *Council* (Comet II), judgment of June 11, 1991, not yet reported (Scope of Article 128).

[42] Case 13/83 *Parliament* v. *Council* [1985] E.C.R. 1513.

Parliament had an equivalent right to seek the annulment of decisions of the Commission or the Council, was satisfied that Article 173 did not confer such a power. The Parliament was not mentioned in that Article, and the Court took the view that no analogy could be drawn with the provisions of Article 175. This decision caused a certain amount of consternation at the time. The Parliament immediately pointed out, in a further case, that the Court's assumption that Parliamentary rights would be protected by the Commission was wrong in circumstances where the Parliament and the Commission disagreed. The Court subsequently accepted that where the privileges and rights of the Parliament were threatened, the Parliament must have power to apply to the Court for a declaration under Article 173 of the Treaty, though it does not have the wider *locus standi* of the Council, the Commission and the Member States to apply even when no direct interest is shown.[43]

It is sometimes said that the Court has not only been "creative" but has played a pivotal role in enhancing the degree of integration which exists in the Community. Was it inevitable that it should work to uphold central government powers against the component units? The Supreme Court of the United States appears to have enhanced the powers of the federal government by taking on judicial review of state laws, by a broad interpretation of the powers given to the federal government, and by rigorously subjecting state laws to the Bill of Rights. On the other hand, it is said that the High Court of Australia and the Supreme Court of Canada until 1982, when the Canadian Act patriating the Constitution and the Charter of Rights and Freedoms was adopted, followed a less teleological, more literal, more traditionally English, role in carrying out statutory

---

[43] Case 302/87 *Parliament* v. *Council* [1988] E.C.R. 5615 and Case 70/88 *Parliament* v. *Council* [1990] E.C.R. I—2024.

interpretation rather than in taking a broader view of the constitutionality of measures in issue before it.

The answer seems to me to be that it was not inevitable but there is no doubt that even without a catalogue of "superior rules" against which constitutionality is to be measured, as was the position of the United States Supreme Court and since 1982, of the Supreme Court of Canada, the Court of Justice has been boldly committed to furthering the aims of the Community as set out in the Preamble to and in Article 2 of the Treaty. It will not be said of the Court, *mutatis mutandis*, as Jefferson said of the judiciary of the United States, that they were "a subtle corps of sappers and miners constantly working underground to undermine the foundations of our confederated fabric." Maybe the European Court's pro-Community bias is "in-built."[44] The fact that it has received the respect of the Governments of the Member States is due in part to the receptiveness and flexibility of national judges who, by conscientiously applying the Court's rulings, have enabled it to continue along the path it embarked upon in the early 1960s.

The Member States *Inter Se*

The Treaty contemplated that there would be disputes between the Member States themselves and that these would be resolved by the Court, particularly since Member States renounced other methods of settlement of their disputes than those provided for in the Treaty.[45] Article 170 enables a Member State to bring before the Court a claim that another Member State has failed to fulfil an obligation under the Treaty. There has only

[44] Joe Rogaly, *Financial Times*, October 15, 1991.
[45] Article 219.

been one such action.[46] Member States may prefer to
quarrel in the Council than in public before the Court
though it is perhaps surprising that more disputes have
not been litigated directly. The answer in part is that it is
more attractive and perhaps simpler for a Member State
to induce the Commission to bring proceedings under
Article 169, alleging a breach of the Treaty and then for
the complainant State to intervene in support of the
Commission, than for the State to begin the proceedings
directly.

It might perhaps have been expected even more that
Member States would have taken advantage of Article
182 of the Treaty by agreeing to submit disputes as to
the subject-matter of the Treaty to the Court. So far no
such submissions have been made. Perhaps the principle
of subsidiarity may provide a basis for such an
agreement.

The individual and the Community

There are not so many direct actions brought before
the Court by individuals since the individual's disputes
normally begin in the national courts and reach the
European Court by way of a reference for a preliminary
ruling. Challenges to a decision addressed to an
individual, or to a regulation or decision addressed to
another person which is of direct and individual concern
to the applicant, can, however, be made on the grounds
open to a Member State. They are relatively common in
relation to decisions that there has been a restrictive
practice or an abuse of a dominant position or a finding
of dumping by a third state and these cases have been of
much importance. There are others where the application of the Community's agricultural policy or the

[46] Case 141/78 *France* v. *United Kingdom* [1979] E.C.R. 2923.

common commercial policy are concerned. Importers of Chilean apples, who were not allowed to bring in apples already on the high seas, gave a recent example[47]—but they are relatively few because of the Court's restrictive interpretation of the phrase "direct and individual concern," an interpretation which could, I believe with advantage, be somewhat relaxed.

The Court has also jurisdiction to hear claims for damages for non-contractual liability[48] and under arbitration clauses contained in a contract concluded by the Community. These are so far very few in number. The latter are to be discouraged not least because the Court is required to decide disputes governed by a national law and not by Community law.

The citizen does not, however, depend on the direct right of access to the Court. Either by way of a preliminary reference or by the decisions of national courts, he has gained rights under Community law, as defined by the Court, and these rights are not limited to those laid down in the regulations and directives adopted by the legislative institutions of the Community. On the contrary, they include fundamental rights recognised by the Court of Justice. In this the Court is unlike the United States Supreme Court (since the Bill of Rights) and the Canadian Supreme Court (since the 1982 Charter), which have specific catalogues of rights. It is in part unlike the Australian High Court where international agreements appear to have led to national legislation conferring specific rights enforceable by the Court. It is also in a position different from the courts of several Member States of the Community whose written constitutions provide for lists of fundamental rights applied by national constitutional courts as a test of the validity of legislation.

---

[47] Case C–152/88 *Sofrimport* v. *Commission* [1990] E.C.R. 2504.
[48] Article 178.

However, and perhaps this is one of the Court's greatest contributions to the development of a Community legal system, after an initial jolt when the German Constitutional Court asserted the primacy of fundamental rights guaranteed by the German Constitution over Community law, the Court has accepted that "respect for fundamental rights forms an integral part of the general principles of law protected"[49] by the Court in ensuring that "in the interpretation and application of this Treaty the law is observed."[50]

Drawing on national constitutions and laws, international treaties and, in particular, the European Convention for the Protection of Human Rights and Fundamental Freedoms, the Court has begun to define those fundamental rights which are to be regarded as part of Community law. They are both procedural and substantive. Thus, in regard to procedure, the Court has insisted on the rule *audi alteram partem*. It has asserted the right to claim privilege for documents passing between a lawyer and his client[51]; the right to protection against unlawful search and seizure[52] (the Commission must comply with certain procedural guarantees) and a limited right against self-incrimination for undertakings subject to investigation by the Commission under Articles 85 and 86 (in replying to questions such companies cannot be compelled, under threat of fine, to admit to a breach of Community law).[53]

On the other hand, rights under the European Convention will only be recognised in an area falling within the sphere of Community action, which usually

---

[49] Case 11/70 *Stauder* [1970] E.C.R. 1125 at 1134.
[50] Article 164.
[51] Case 155/79 *A.M. & S. Europe* [1982] E.C.R. 1575.
[52] Joined Cases 46/87 and 227/88 *Hoechst* [1989] E.C.R. 2859.
[53] Case 374/87 *Orkem* [1989] E.C.R. 3283.

means in an economic context. The way in which a question can arise is well illustrated by the case of *Grogan*,[54] which reveals how sensitive can be the issues coming before the Court.

Abortion is prohibited in Ireland and the right to life of the unborn is recognised by the Constitution.[55] Officers of students' associations distributed details of the availability of abortion clinics in the United Kingdom. Proceedings were brought against them for a declaration that to distribute such information was unlawful. Questions were referred to the European Court, which ruled, in answer to the contention that abortion was grossly immoral so that it could not be a service, that the termination of pregnancy was a medical activity usually performed for remuneration, which can be carried out as a professional activity. It was, therefore, a service within the meaning of Article 59 of the Treaty. The act of the students' officers in distributing information was so far removed from the abortions carried out in clinics in another Member State that the prohibition on distribution could not be considered a restriction within the meaning of Article 59. Moreover, reliance could not be placed upon the European Convention of Human Rights ("the observance of which the Court ensures") since the national legislation in question lay outside the scope of European Community law. Thus, the Convention is recognised to apply only in cases where Community law applies. The Court did not decide that a restriction on clinics from another Member State distributing leaflets in Ireland about their own activities would not be in breach of Community law.

---

[54] Case C–159/90 *The Society for the Protection of Unborn Children Ireland Ltd.* v. *Grogan and others*, judgment of October 4, 1991, not yet reported.
[55] Article 40, s.3.

That remains an open question, though the wording of the judgment may give some indication.

Three major principles of Community law are regularly cited to the Court in one context or another: proportionality, legitimate expectations and legal certainty.

Whereas an English court will confine itself to asking whether any reasonable administrative body could have come to the decision under attack, the Court of Justice asks itself whether the measure in question is "proportionate" to its stated aims and objectives. This requires it to consider whether the measure actually achieves or is likely to achieve the end claimed for it, whether or not a measure less restrictive of individual freedom would achieve the same result and finally, whether the objective of the measure justifies even that minimum level of interference with individual liberty.[56] Both the doctrine of proportionality and the criterion of reasonableness call for value judgments as to what is "justifiable" or "reasonable" but the Court of Justice has, in addition, to undertake the difficult task of assessing the likely effect of hypothetical alternatives to the measure under examination.[57]

Under the heading of legitimate expectations,[58] the Court protects the right of prudent and discriminating

---

[56] See, for example, Case 331/88 *R.* v. *Ministry of Agriculture, Fisheries and Food ex parte Fedesa* [1990] E.C.R. 4057.

[57] For differing conclusions as to whether an impugned measure was either necessary or appropriate, compare the Advocate-General's Opinion and the judgment of the Court in Case 302/86 *Commission* v. *Denmark* [1988] E.C.R. 4627 (the *Danish Bottles* case).

[58] See Lord Mackenzie Stuart, "Legitimate Expectations and Estoppel in Community Law and English Administrative Law" (1983) Legal Issues in European Integration 53; Hubeau, "Le principe de la protection de la confiance légitime dans la jurisprudence de la Cour de justice des communautés européennes" (1983) Cahier de Dr.Eur. 143; Sharpston, "Legitimate Expectations and Economic Reality" (1990) 11 E.L.Rev. 103.

traders to rely on justifiable assumptions as to the continued existence of a given legal situation. Reliance on the doctrine of legitimate expectations, unlike reliance on estoppel, does not require the applicant to show that he was given positive assurances, either express or implied, as to the future policy of the Communities. The Court will determine whether the expectations of the trader were "legitimate" or "reasonable" from an examination of all the circumstances of the case.[59] An expectation will not be legitimate where the individuals concerned were forewarned of impending changes to the rules[60] or where the situation in question is necessarily or usually subject to uncertainties.[61]

The principle of legal certainty generally precludes the adoption of measures having retroactive effects although the Court will countenance such measures provided that the purpose to be achieved so demands it and the legitimate expectations of those concerned are duly respected.[62] The principle of legal certainty also requires that any rule imposing charges on the tax-payer[63] or imposing a penalty, even of a non-criminal nature,[64] must be clear and precise.

Interim Relief

Sometimes the Court is called upon to make an immediate order under its powers to suspend the application of a contested act or "in cases before it to

---

[59] See Case 289/81 *Mavridis* v. *Parliament* [1983] E.C.R. 1731.
[60] See Case 97/76 *Merkur* v. *Commission* [1977] E.C.R. 1063.
[61] Case 146/77 *British Beef Company* v. *Intervention Board for Agricultural Produce* [1978] E.C.R. 1347.
[62] Case C–337/88 *SAFA* [1990] E.C.R. I—1.
[63] Case 169/80 *Administration des Douanes* v. *Gondrad Frères* [1981] E.C.R. 1931.
[64] Case 117/83 *Könecke* v. *Balm* [1984] E.C.R. 3291.

prescribe any necessary interim measures." The procedure here is very expeditious. Usually there is time for both sides to put in written observations but occasionally an order has been made on a temporary basis even before the opponent has had a chance to reply to the application. In any case the hearing takes place quickly, usually before the President of the Court or a judge appointed by him, the judge reporter and the advocate-general. After a short hearing the written decision is communicated to the parties within a few days. Even if there is not the sense of urgency or drama which sometimes surrounds an *ex parte* application to a judge in England, important issues can be at stake. There is a difference in procedure which to some extent affects the atmosphere since the presiding judge normally opens the discussion and limits counsel to dealing with what he, the presiding judge, sees as the relevant issues. Witnesses are rare and there is usually no more than an informal debate. Before an order is made the Court must be satisfied that there is a clearly arguable case for the grant of interim measures (a *"fumus boni juris"*), that there is urgency in the sense that if no immediate order is made damage which cannot be sufficiently compensated in money will occur before the Court can make a final order and that the order made does not prejudice any decision at the final hearing.

Two recent cases show how interests have to be balanced. In one the Commission sought to prevent construction work in an area protected as the habitat of migratory birds. It was said that this construction work would cause the loss of the natural habitat. As a interim measure, relief was refused because the Commission had delayed and the remaining work was unlikely to cause serious harm to the birds.[65]

[65] Case C–57/89R *Commission* v. *Germany* [1989] E.C.R. 2849.

In the second case, an application was made to prevent the coming into effect of German legislation imposing a toll on lorry drivers using the motorways. This was said to be discriminatory because the road tax on German lorries was reduced by an amount approximately equal to the toll, so that only drivers from other States would pay an extra amount. Despite arguments that these tolls were urgently needed for environmental purposes, an interim order was made that the legislation should not be put into effect because of the likely serious damage to small road haulage contractors in other Member States.[66]

The Court is very cautious before granting relief though the burden upon an applicant to show a sufficient case has varied from time to time. Without wishing to encourage unnecessary or feeble applications, it does seem to me that there is some room here for development of this jurisdiction both before the Court and the Court of First Instance even though, compared with the kind of cases which come before a national court, there is clearly less scope in the European Court for the use of these interim measures.

Conclusion

And so, the Community with federal features if not a federation, has a Court with limited jurisdiction but effective powers of judicial review, with tools to ensure that Member States are kept up to the mark even if there is no power to enforce its decisions, and with an essentially efficient procedure for achieving consistency in the application of Community law. Its competence to lay down general principles of law is wholly accepted; its willingness to exercise that function is not only evident

[66] Case C–195/90R *Commission* v. *Germany* [1990] E.C.R. I—2715.

but highly influential in the development of the Community.

2. EFFECTING A MARKET

Two striking features of the Treaty of Rome are at times the generality, at times the brevity, of many of its provisions. Each of these features was capable of exerting a radical influence on the role of the Court, charged as it was with the task of ensuring that in the interpretation and application of the Treaty the law is observed. The opportunity was there, if the Court were willing to take it, of ensuring that the provisions of the Treaty itself, and of subordinate legislation made pursuant to it, were interpreted and applied in such a way that the aims of the Community were fully achieved.

A striking feature of the Court's record over the years is the extent to which it has seized this opportunity, not merely by its interpretation of the words actually used, but also by its realisation of what was inherently necessary if its aims were to be achieved. This was done, in part, by the declaration of general principles of law, but also, and of no less importance, by the Court's recognition that specific provisions of the Treaty had to be fleshed out either to make those provisions work effectively or to adapt them to the different situations existing at various stages of the Community's development.

The practice of the Court in interpreting Community legislation derives from this recognition. Most of us, after accession, adopted, or perhaps even learned, the word "teleological" as a principle of interpretation and we were told that it was very different from the "literal" approach of the English judge. I think that difference is sometimes exaggerated[1] though it does exist. Because the Treaty is largely a framework, and because the Treaty and subordinate legislation are to be read in several equally authentic languages and to be applied to twelve different States, there is no doubt that the task of interpretation is very different from that in national law so that the "object and purpose" and the "context" of a provision may sometimes override the literal interpretation, which in itself may seem clear.[2] The various language versions must be interpreted in a uniform way and if there is a divergence then the words must be construed in accordance with the purpose and general scheme of the legislation of which they form part. The approach of the Court to the work of interpretation was clearly explained by one of its former Presidents:

"The special nature of the Community, which must be regarded, not as an association of States subject to international law, but as a community *sui generis* orientated to the future and designed with a view to the alteration of economic and social relationships and progressive integration, rules out a static and requires

---

[1] Lord Wilberforce in *Black Clawson* v. *Papierwerke* said that if a task of judicial construction is to be properly done it must be "related to such matters as intelligibility to the citizen, constitutional propriety, consideration of history, comity of nations, reasonable and non-retroactive effect and, no doubt, in some contexts to social needs . . . It is sound enough to ascertain, if that can be done, the objectives of any particular meaning." [1975] 1 All E.R. 810, 818.

[2] See the excellent note by Timothy Millett, "Rules of Interpretation of E.E.C. Legislation" (1989) Statute Law Review, p. 163.

a dynamic and evolutionary interpretation of Community law. The Community judge must never forget that the Treaties establishing the European Communities have laid the foundations of an ever closer union among the peoples of Europe and that the High Contracting Parties were anxious to strengthen the unity of their economies and to ensure their harmonious development (Preamble to the E.E.C. Treaty). The principle of the progressive integration of the Member States in order to attain the objectives of the Treaty does not only comprise a political requirement; it amounts rather to a Community legal principle, which the Court of Justice has to bear in mind when interpreting Community law, if it is to discharge in a proper manner its allotted task of upholding the law when it interprets and applies the Treaties. How else should the Court of Justice carry out this function which it has been assigned except by an interpretation of Community law geared to the aims of the Treaty, that is to say, one which is dynamic and teleological."[3]

That process has undoubtedly resulted in the Court making a significant contribution to European integration. Those who approve call it "creative"; those who disapprove refer to legislation or government by judges. Neither of these descriptions is really accurate if "creative" implies going beyond what the founding fathers set out to build and if "legislation" or "government" imply decisions based wholly on political policy. Constructive, however, the process has certainly been, not least in the achievement of results clearly intended

[3] H. Kutscher, "Methods of Interpretation as seen by a Judge at the Court of Justice," p. 37, Judicial and Academic Conference September 17–28, (1976), Court of Justice of the European Communities.

by the Treaty, where legislation which ought to have been adopted had not been adopted. It is equally constructive in the way Community rules have been applied to changing circumstances. The process was, however, not just "constructive" in the sense that the Court has built upon its own concept of what should be done; it was essential if the Community was to be effective given the type of Treaty which was adopted.

The creation of a customs union (with a common external tariff and commercial policy in relation to non-Member countries) as opposed to a free trade area, and a common market, with the economic policies of the Member States progressively approximated, underlay the Community target of what is, essentially, a free market economy. The extent to which the Court has contributed to that economic integration can be illustrated in many ways. I shall select three areas in the field of trade: (a) the creation of the common market; (b) the functioning of the common market; and (c) the common market and international trade.

A. FUNDAMENTAL STEPS IN CREATING A COMMON MARKET

Overturning barriers

If the common market was ever to become a reality it was clearly essential that full effect should be given to those articles of the Treaty which strike down barriers to trade and which outlaw discriminatory measures.

Thus, in the first place, discriminatory taxes had to go; ingenious excuses for such taxes being rejected. The Court led the way by laying down the rule that, in deciding whether internal taxation in one Member State is in excess of that imposed directly or indirectly on "similar domestic products,"[4] it is necessary "to interpret the concept of 'similar products' with sufficient flexibility."[5] The definition of "similar products" as those which "have similar characteristics and meet the same needs from the point of view of consumers" may seem general. It leaves much for the national judge to assess but, at the same time, tackles the real problem whilst leaving scope for a consideration of the varied customs and tastes of the inhabitants of the different Member States. Sometimes the matter is so clear that the Court itself can effectively decide the issue. It did so when it found that Scotch whisky and French cognac were similar products to Italian-made grappa, which bore a tax in Italy which was lower than that imposed on the imported products.[6] Inventive arguments about satisfying different tastes at different social levels simply could not be allowed to succeed in order to justify a clearly discriminatory tax.

In the second place, and of more significance, because liable to give rise to greater abuses, were the prohibitions (a) on *charges* having equivalent effect to customs duties (which later were themselves prohibited and which disappeared early giving the Court few or no problems)[7] and (b) on *measures* having equivalent effect to quantitative restrictions on imports (which later were also prohibited and which did not in practice need any sophisticated definition).[8]

The definitions given by the Court to the concepts of "charges having equivalent effect" and of "measures having equivalent effect" are extensive. As applied by

[4] Article 95.
[5] Case 168/78 *France*, Case 169/78 *Italy*, Case 170/78 *United Kingdom*, Case 171/78 *Denmark* [1980] E.C.R. 347, 385, 417, 447 respectively.
[6] Case 319/81 *Commission* v. *Italy* [1983] E.C.R. 601.
[7] Article 12.
[8] Article 30.

the Court, these concepts have had more influence on the creation of the common market than any other branch of the Court's jurisprudence and perhaps as much influence as anything done by way of subordinate legislation.

Thus, a charge having equivalent effect to a customs duty is defined as:

> "any pecuniary charge, however small, and whatever its designation and mode of application, which is imposed unilaterally on domestic or foreign goods by reason of the fact that they cross a frontier and which is not a customs duty in the strict sense ... even if it is not imposed for the benefit of the State, is not discriminatory or protective in effect and if the product on which the charge is imposed is not in competition with any domestic produce."[9]

The crucial elements are hence that the charges should be imposed unilaterally—thus excluding charges for genuine services contractually agreed; and that they should be imposed by reason of the fact that the goods cross a frontier—thus excluding taxes imposed subsequently or for some other reason, even if the goods have crossed a frontier. Not all charges imposed on goods which have been imported or exported are therefore caught by the definition. However, exemptions on the basis of overriding national or economic reasons cannot be relied on to justify exemptions. The Treaty does not so provide. The Court has not recognised the possibility of such exemptions.[10]

It is, however, the definition of a "measure having equivalent effect to a quantitative restriction on imports"

---

[9] Case 24/68 *Commission* v. *Italy* [1969] E.C.R. 193.
[10] Case 266/81 *SIOT* [1983] E.C.R. 731.

which has had the greatest effect and which continues to give rise to important and difficult cases,[11] some of them touching upon very sensitive national nerves and prejudices such as the traditional restriction on the appellation "beer" to products made in accordance with a German law based on an old Bavarian law of 1516,[12] or the restriction on the sale in Italy of pasta not made in accordance with the Italian requirement that only durum wheat should be used to make pasta.[13]

Once again, the Court's definition is very wide—

"all trading rules enacted by Member States which are capable of hindering directly or indirectly, actually or potentially, intra-Community trade are to be considered as measures having an effect equivalent to quantitative restrictions."[14]

"Capable of hindering," "indirectly," "potentially" give the key to the firmness with which the Court has sought to interpret and apply Article 30. The net sweeps very wide.

In later cases, beginning with *Cassis de Dijon*,[15] the Court opened up a new and more general approach by recognising a principle of equivalence according to which, where a product has been lawfully produced and marketed in one Member State, it must be allowed to be traded freely throughout the Community.

That decision has had a great effect. When it was given, the laws of the Member States contained many

[11] In Articles 12 and 34 there are parallel provisions dealing with exports, the latter having led to some distinctions with Article 30.

[12] Case 178/84 *Commission* v. *Germany* [1987] E.C.R. 1227.

[13] Case 407/85 *Glocken GmbH and Kritzinger* v. *USL Centro sud et Provincia Autonome di Bolzano* [1988] E.C.R. 4233.

[14] Case 8/74 *Dassonville* [1974] E.C.R. 837.

[15] Case 120/78 *Rewe-Zentrale AG* [1979] E.C.R. 649.

provisions which were capable of restricting trade. Some of them appeared, prima facie, to be for justifiable purposes. It was, however, obviously desirable to harmonise these national rules as to content, quality and packaging so that products could move freely around the Community. To achieve this result there was even talk of laying down Community definitions for various food-stuffs, hence the jokes in the press about a Community loaf and a Community sausage. Yet, to harmonise all these national rules so as to enable goods to move around subject to justified restrictions, even in relation to foodstuffs, was an enormous administrative and legislative task, which the Commission had only just begun to tackle. The judgment in *Cassis de Dijon* allowed goods to move around if they could be lawfully produced and marketed in one Member State, thus, in the eyes of the Commission, making it unnecessary to have specific legislation harmonising rules as to these goods. They could circulate even without such legislation.

It followed from this decision that national rules could not be allowed to prohibit the use in one Member State of wine bottles of a particular shape lawfully produced and used in another Member State,[16] or require round packages to be used exclusively for margarine and square packages exclusively for butter,[17] or prohibit the sale of gin from one Member State because it has a different alcoholic content to the gin produced in the Member State applying the prohibition.[18]

With some exceptions

The *Cassis de Dijon* decision, however, has a wider import which has not yet been fully developed.

[16] Case 16/83 *Prantl* [1984] E.C.R. 1299.
[17] Case 261/81 *Rau* v. *De Smedt* [1982] E.C.R. 3961.
[18] Case 182/84 *Miro B.V.* [1985] E.C.R. 3731.

The German Government, in that case, argued that the prohibition on the import of liqueurs with a strength of less than 25 per cent. was justified, *inter alia*, in the interests of health and of preventing the purchaser from being confused as to what he was buying.

Should this kind of justification be allowed to cut down the prohibition of measures having equivalent effect to quantitative restrictions?

That rule is subject to exceptions set out in the Treaty itself, since prohibitions or restrictions on imports or exports

> "justified on grounds of public morality, public policy or public security; the protection of health and life of humans, animals or plants; the protection of national treasures possessing artistic, historic or archaeological value; or the protection of industrial and commercial property" are not precluded provided that they do not "constitute a means of arbitrary discrimination or a disguised restriction on trade between Member States."[19]

It might well have been thought that, with this express provision in Article 36 of the Treaty, it was clear that these were the only limitations to the prohibition, all the more so since the Court itself had rules that further items could not be added to the list of exceptions in that Article.[20]

The Court, however, recognised in *Cassis de Dijon* that, at that stage of the Community's development, and in the absence of common rules relating to the production

[19] Article 36.
[20] Case 113/80 *Commission* v. *Ireland* ("Irish Souvenirs") [1981] E.C.R. 1625.

and marketing of alcohol, it was for each Member State to regulate such matters in its own territory. Thus:

> "obstacles to movement within the Community resulting from disparities between the national laws ... must be accepted in so far as those provisions may be recognised as being necessary in order to satisfy mandatory requirements relating in particular to the effectiveness of fiscal supervision, the protection of public health, the fairness of commercial transactions and the defence of the consumer."[21]

I have never found the phrase "mandatory requirements" particularly helpful. I am not sure if the French "exigence impérative" is any clearer. However "mandatory requirements" seems to be hallowed by time even if it does not explain that a rule must be justified as well as obligatory.

Obstacles contained in national rules are in any event only justifiable on the basis of a mandatory requirement where they apply without distinction to the Member State's own goods and to imported goods. Restrictions applicable only to imported goods have often been rejected on the ground that they constitute discriminatory measures.[22] Mandatory requirements can be relied on, moreover, only where national laws have not been harmonised. They are not to be seen as an exception to Article 30 in the sense of the Article 36 exceptions but as a recognition that certain matters remain under national jurisdiction pending the adoption of Community legislation. To that extent they are of a temporary nature. On the other hand, the list of "mandatory requirements" is not closed, unlike the list of exceptions in Article 36.

[21] Case 120/78, *supra*.
[22] Case 113/80, *supra*, and Case 434/85 *Allen and Hanburys Ltd.* v. *Generics* [1988] E.C.R. 1245.

Since the judgment in *Cassis de Dijon*, the Court has, for example, recognised that environmental and cultural considerations may justify national restrictions and it is perfectly possible that with the passage of time, circumstances will show that further mandatory requirements by Member States are justified.[23] That will be for the Court to decide.

It is perhaps, at first sight, curious that the Article 36 exceptions should be construed restrictively whereas the class of mandatory requirements can be defined and extended by the Court even though the Court has insisted both that a clear need for such measures is established and that the principle of proportionality is observed. It is also curious that the Court, in listing mandatory requirements, should have included the protection of public health. Article 36 itself already refers to "the protection of the health and life of humans" as being an exception to the prohibition in Article 30. It seems doubtful whether any distinction was really intended between these two categories, in which case the mandatory requirement in respect of the protection of public health seems unnecessary and even wrong in principle.[24] On this point, it is to be noted that, in *Beele*,[25] the Advocate General considered a restriction on the basis of Article 36, whereas the Court relied exclusively on the concept of mandatory requirements, to justify an exception. The Court has not specifically dealt with this apparent overlap but has avoided the issue by saying that, if a restriction is covered by Article 36, is is unnecessary to deal with the question of

---

[23] Joined Cases 60–61/84 *Cinéthèque SA* v. *Fédération nationale des cinémas français* [1985] E.C.R. 2605 and Case 302/86 *Commission* v. *Denmark* [1988] E.C.R. 4607.

[24] *Cf.* Joined Cases 1 and 176/90 *Aragonesa de Publicidad Exterior*, judgment of July 25, 1991, not yet reported.

[25] Case 6/81 *Industrie Diensten Groep* v. *Beele* [1982] E.C.R. 1625.

mandatory requirements.[26] It may one day have to be resolved. It is perhaps just as well to rely on the Treaty when the words are there and to leave the overlap with any item in the list of mandatory requirements, if there is such an overlap, to fall into desuetude.

Sometimes, when the question arises as to whether mandatory requirements are justified, economic and political factors merge. Thus in *Campus Oil*,[27] where the Irish Government required importers to purchase a proportion of their requirements of petroleum products from a State-owned refinery situated in Ireland, at a price to be defined by the Government, there was clearly a measure of equivalent effect to a quantitative restriction. When public security was relied on as a justification, the Court took notice of political and economic factors linked to the existence of a sufficient oil supply for a modern state and said:

"In the light of the seriousness of the consequences that an interruption in supplies of petroleum products may have for a country's existence, the aim of ensuring a minimum supply of petroleum products at all times is to be regarded as transcending purely economic considerations and thus as capable of constituting an objective covered by the concept of public security."

Two of the other freedoms relating to the movement of persons set out in the Treaty, the freedom of establishment and the freedom to provide services, are also, by Article 56, subject to exceptions. These recognise that restrictions on foreign nationals on the grounds of public

[26] Case C–288/89 *Stichting Collectieve Antennevoorziening Gouda and others* v. *Commissariaat voor de Media*, judgment of July 25, 1991, not yet reported.
[27] Case 72/83 *Campus Oil Ltd.* [1984] E.C.R. 2727.

policy, public security or public health may be justified.

Though there were, in the past, suggestions that the notion of mandatory requirements could be applied to the provision of services,[28] there was no clear decision to that effect until *Gouda*,[29] where restrictions on advertising on Dutch television were in question. There, the Court accepted that restrictions which were not discriminatory could, in principle, be justified by reference to mandatory requirements, but found that restrictions in that particular case could not be justified in the interests of cultural policy or pluralism of languages. Nor were the restrictions on advertising justified in the circumstances of the case, even though some restriction on the duration and frequency of such publicity might be justified in the interests of protecting the consumer.

Cassis de Dijon has thus been a case of great importance and, although well known, is as good an illustration as any, for Miss Hamlyn's purposes, of the effect of the Court's involvement in the creation of the market and, therefore, of its impact on English law and English commerce. The name of the case will certainly be found to be engraved on the hearts of the judges who have sat in Luxembourg. The first dinner of the Court which I attended in Luxembourg was preceded by a glass of "Kir" for the sole reason that Kir contains the liqueur, Cassis de Dijon, and it seemed appropriate to do homage to the judgment in that case.

Free movement and the protection of property rights in the market

These were not, however, the only problems raised by Article 30 and Article 36 in connection with the creation

---

[28] Case 279/80 *Webb* [1981] E.C.R. 3305.
[29] Case 288/89 *Gouda, supra.*

of the common market. Difficult problems have arisen in relation to the protection of industrial and commercial property. It was thus, for example, necessary to reconcile the prohibition of restrictions on the free movement of goods with the provision in Article 36 that Article 30 did not preclude prohibitions or restrictions on imports "justified on the grounds of the protection of industrial and commercial property" and the provision "that the Treaty shall in no way prejudice the rules in Member States governing the system of property ownership."[30]

The Court began by drawing a distinction between the existence of commercial property rights and their exercise, holding that Community law may have an effect on their exercise even if their existence is entirely a matter for national law.[31] Some commentators found the initial solutions of the Court to be incomplete or unsatisfactory. What, for example, is the difference between existence and exercise? What is an abuse in the exercise of rights for Community law purposes? What are the boundaries between national law rights and Treaty obligations?

The Court concentrated on the specific object of the rights concerned and developed a theory of the exhaustion of rights. If a patentee markets his products in a Member State where the law does not provide patent protection, he must then accept the principle of the free movement of goods.[32] "The proprietor of an industrial or commercial property right protected by the law of a Member State cannot rely on that law to prevent

---

[30] Article 222.

[31] Case 24/67 *Parke Davis* [1968] E.C.R. 55; Case 40/70 *Sirena* [1971] E.C.R. 69.

[32] Case 15/74 *Centrafarm* v. *Sterling Drug* [1974] E.C.R. 1147, Case 102/77 *Hoffman La Roche* [1978] E.C.R. 1139, 187/80 *Merck Stephan* [1981] E.C.R. 2063, 19/84 *Pharmon* [1985] E.C.R. 2281, 193/83 *Windsurfing International* [1986] E.C.R. 611.

the importation of a product which has been lawfully marketed in another Member State by the proprietor himself or with his consent."[33] Here the principle of the free movement of goods contained in Article 30 is overriding. However, this principle is only applicable where the owner of the patent right has willingly given his consent to the circulation of the product.

The relationship between the protection of industrial and commercial property rights and the free movement of goods has also been a matter of difficulty in relation to trade marks. Here again a distinction was drawn between the existence and the exercise of a trade mark.[34] The "specific subject matter" of the trade mark right was recognised to be

"the guarantee that the owner of the trade mark has the exclusive right to use that trade mark, for the purpose of putting products protected by the trade mark into circulation for the first time, and is therefore intended to protect him against competitors wishing to take advantage of the status and reputation of the trade mark by selling products illegally bearing that trade mark."[35]

At the same time: "The exercise, by the owner of a trade mark, of the right which he enjoys under the legislation of a Member State to prohibit the sale, in that State, of a product which has been marketed under the trade mark in another Member State by the trade mark owner or with his consent is incompatible with the rule of the EEC Treaty concerning the free movement of goods" within the Community.

[33] Case 119/75 *Terrapin* [1976] E.C.R. 1039, Joined Cases 55 & 57/80 *Musik-Vertrieb Membran* and *K-tel* [1981] E.C.R. 147.

[34] Case 40/70 *Sirena, supra.*

[35] Case 16/74 *Centrafarm* v. *Winthrop* [1974] E.C.R. 1183.

The difficulty is shown by the decisions of the Court in relation to the decaffeinated coffee, "Hag," which was the subject of trade marks in Germany and Belgium before the First World War. Following sequestration and resale of the German trade marks after the Second World War, the German and Belgian marks became vested in two different companies. When the German company marketed its products in the Benelux countries, an action was brought against it for infringement of the Belgian trade mark.

In its first ruling in 1974,[36] the Court held that to prohibit the marketing in one Member State of a product legally bearing a trade mark in another Member State for the sole reason that an identical trade mark, having the same origin, exists in the first State, is incompatible with Article 30.

However, the Court has recently reconsidered that interpretation. The Belgian Hag company became a wholly-owned subsidiary of a Swiss company and began to import into Germany the decaffeinated coffee Hag manufactured in Belgium. An action was brought before the German Courts in order to prevent such importation because the German company maintained that Kaffee Hag had the status of a famous brand and that its product was superior in quality by virtue of a new manufacturing process.[37]

The Court expressly reversed its previous ruling. The essential function of a trade mark was recognised to be that of guaranteeing to the consumer the origin of the product. That function would be compromised if the holder of the trade mark could not prevent the importation of a similar product under a name which could be confused with its own mark. This analysis is

---

[36] Case 192/73 *Van Zuylen* v. *Hag* [1974] E.C.R. 731.
[37] Case C–10/89 *SA CNL-Sucal NV* v. *Hag* [1990] E.C.R. I–3711.

not affected by the fact that the trade marks in this case originally belonged to the same holder who had been dispossessed following the post-war expropriation. On the contrary, from the time of that expropriation and despite their common origin, these trade marks were independent of each other and each mark, in its particular territorial area, had the role of guaranteeing that the products bearing the trade mark came from a single source.

As the Court put it, the Treaty does

"not preclude national legislation from allowing an undertaking which is the holder of a trade mark in a Member State from opposing the importation from another Member State of similar products lawfully bearing an identical trade mark in the latter State or liable to confusion with the protected mark even though the mark under which the contested products are imported originally belonged to a subsidiary of the undertaking which opposes the importation and was acquired by a third undertaking as a result of the expropriation of that subsidiary."

The result of the second judgment clearly answers many of the criticisms levelled against the first *Hag* judgment.[38] It may, however, still raise questions—some of which were included in the submissions made to the Court—as to whether the sharing agreement, the sequestration and its effects were given the right weight. In the two Member States in question trade mark rights prevail; *quaere* whether in other States different products can be marketed under the same trade mark by both the

[38] See F. A. Mann, Industrial Property and the EEC Treaty, (1975) ICLQ No. 1, p. 31; although compare F. G. Jacobs, Industrial Property and the EEC Treaty: A Reply, (1975) ICLQ, No. 4, p. 643.

German and the Belgian holders of the trade mark. It is, however, to be noted that, in the last paragraph of the judgment, the Court seeks to put right, for the future, the position in Belgium in relation to importations from Germany in order to avoid the need for the parties to make a further application to the Court.

The difficulty of applying Article 30 in intellectual property cases is illustrated by two applications currently pending before the Court.[39] The cases concern the system applied in the United Kingdom and Italy which permits compulsory licences to be granted where the patented invention is not being "worked to the fullest extent that is reasonably practicable." Under the relevant United Kingdom legislation the patent is deemed not to be reasonably worked if a demand for the product is not being met or if such demand is being met to a substantial extent by importation. The Commission has argued that this system is contrary to Article 30. Essentially its argument is that a holder of a United Kingdom patent who wishes to preserve exclusivity, and who will therefore have to ensure that demand for the product is being met on reasonable terms in the United Kingdom, will be encouraged to base his production in the United Kingdom rather than to satisfy demand by importing from another Member State. This is due to the fact that, under the national legislation, satisfying demand by importation is not equated to domestic production. The United Kingdom replies that the whole purpose of granting a patent has always been to encourage local innovation and production. Indeed, all the Member States, with the exception of the Benelux countries, have similar legislation, although France, Greece and Ireland have now undertaken to amend theirs following the threat of infringement proceedings.

[39] Case C–235/89 *Commission* v. *Italy* and Case C–30/90 *Commission* v. *United Kingdom*, pending.

Infringement proceedings have been commenced against Denmark, Germany, Portugal and Spain.

As with all intellectual property cases arising in the context of Community law, these cases raise the difficult and delicate task of attempting to reconcile the broad and vitally important principle of the free movement of goods and non-discrimination between domestic production and imports from Community countries with the goal of patent legislation which is intended precisely to give a certain amount of encouragement and protection to domestic production.

A common agricultural policy for the market

Article 30 has had no lesser effect on the establishment of common organisations of the market in the Community. The common agricultural policy, covering the products of the soil, animals and fish, has been operated largely through market organisations and is the most developed of all the Community's policies, however much criticised. Since one of the tasks of the Court is to review the legality of legislation introduced by the Council and the Commission, it was important to ensure that basic principles of the Treaty were not violated.

The "extensive powers granted to the Community institutions in the conduct" of the agricultural policy "must be exercised from the perspective of the unity of the market to the exclusion of any measure compromising the abolition between Member States of customs duties and quantitative restrictions or charges or measures having equivalent effect. Any prejudice to what the Community has achieved in relation to the unity of the market moreover risks opening the way to mechanisms which would lead to distintegration contrary to the objectives of progressive approximation of the economic policies of the Member States set out in Article 2 of the Treaty."[40]

In some agricultural products, including potatoes, cotton and wood, no common organisation of the market has been established and Member States have continued their own national market organisations. The Court, however, has stated unequivocally that such a national organisation cannot avoid the application of rules concerning the free movement of goods.[41] As Mr. Advocate General Mayras said, this principle constitutes "the adoption of a position which is intended to exert pressure on the Community executive and, through it, on the Member States in order to ensure that the Treaty is applied to the full."[42]

Member States may thus take measures in regard to national market organisations so long as they do not alter the market structure of the Community or jeopardise the aims and functioning of the market and, in particular, do not impede intra-Community trade.[43] Obstacles to free movement may however be acceptable to correct distortions and restore competitive equality between producers in exceptional circumstances. Their scope must be limited to their specific objective in the context of bringing about market conditions which come closest to those of an internal market.[44] For this reason

---

[40] Joined Cases 80 and 81/77 *Commissaires réunis* v. *Receveur des douanes* [1978] E.C.R. 927 at 947.

[41] Case 48/74 *Charmasson* [1974] E.C.R. 1383, noted by D. Wyatt (1976) European Law Review, p. 310 and Case 68/76 *Commission* v. *France* [1977] E.C.R. 515 at 531.

[42] Case 117/78 *Meijer* v. *Department of Trade* [1979] E.C.R. 1387 at 1419.

[43] Case 31/74 *Galli* [1975] E.C.R. 45 and Case 154/77 *Dechmann* [1978] E.C.R. 1563.

[44] Joined Cases 40–48, 50, 54–56, 111, 113 and 114/73 *Suiker Unie and others* v. *Commission* [1975] E.C.R. 1663 and Case 61/86 *United Kingdom* v. *Commission* [1988] E.C.R. 431.

too, as a short term economic policy measure, monetary compensatory amounts (levies or subsidies) were accepted. These were designed to compensate for the different price levels prevailing in the different Member States in respect of agricultural products, and which resulted from fluctuations in the exchange rates of national currencies. Although the Court left much in this area to the discretion of the Commission, it was stressed that the Commission must "always ensure that the application of monetary compensatory amounts is limited to what is strictly necessary in order to neutralise the effects of currency fluctuations between the Member States."[45]

In *Aliments Morvan*,[46] the Court held that the common agricultural policy prevents a Member State from imposing a tax on a limited number of agricultural products over a long period, which might have the effect of leading economic operators to change the structure of their production or consumption.

These cases relating to the common agricultural policy show that the Court has insisted firmly on the basic principles of the Treaty whilst realistically accepting temporary derogations without in any sense trespassing on the functions of the legislature.[47]

The free movement of goods is, of course, only one aspect of the common market. It is the first of the foundations of the Community to be dealt with in the Treaty. The free movement of persons, services and capital are also important "foundations" and, particularly

---

[45] Case 79/77 *Kühlhaus-Zentrum* v. *Hauptzollamt Hamburg-Harburg* [1978] E.C.R. 611.
[46] Case C–235/90 *SARL Aliments Morvan*, judgment of November 19, 1991, not yet reported.
[47] Case 253/84 *GAEC de la Ségaude* v. *Council and Commission* [1987] E.C.R. 123.

in relation to services, are in the process of or on the verge of substantial further development.

B. THE FUNCTIONING OF THE COMMON MARKET

The competition rules

There are, however, in addition to the "foundations," sections of the Treaty dealing with "the policy" of the Community—rules on competition and State aids by Member States themselves; on economic and commercial policy, including restraints on dumping by outside countries; on social policy; and now, under the Single European Act, on environmental policy, research and technological development.

All these in one way or another relate to the creation of the common market. I mention only one aspect, one which has most often concerned the Court and which is now a matter for the Court of First Instance. This relates to the competition rules, which are an essential ancillary of the creation of the common market and the free movement of goods and which the Court has undoubtedly tended to interpret and apply against that background.

The object of the Treaty was not only to create a common market but also to adopt rules which would allow the free market to function. In this respect, Article 3(f), which aims at the institution of a system ensuring that competition in the common market is not distorted, is crucial. Striking down State-made barriers helped to free competition: barriers maintained by undertakings or by national rules in relation to trade practices which would distort competition had to go. Freeing competition, however, is not only relevant in relation to the free movement of goods. It is relevant to other activities. When new regulations are adopted in a particular sector of Community commerce (for example, transport or banking), the Council may adopt a regulation concerning competition in that sector.[48] These competition rules affect not only the traders themselves, they are also relevant for the protection of consumers' interests, for the improvement of distribution systems and for technical improvements.

The subject is complex and extensive and I do no more than illustrate how the Court has added to the skeleton of Articles 85 and 86 of the Treaty in ways which are relevant to the creation of the common market.

In the first place, the Court has recognised that restrictive practices and abuses of a dominant position, which are subject to Treaty control, are not limited to acts done to and by companies present in the territory of the Community. Thus, "the fact that one of the undertakings which are parties to the agreement is situated in a third country does not prevent application of that provision since the agreement is operative on the territory of the common market."[49] Moreover, undertakings are to be seen in terms of economic or commercial reality rather than with regard solely to their legal personality. The "veil" has been lifted in cases where the existence of a legally independent subsidiary conceals

[48] For example, Regulation 4056/86 on maritime transport, O.J. (1986) L.378; Regulations 3975/87 and 3976/87 on air transport, O.J. (1987) L.374; Regulation 1017/68 on haulage, railways and inland water transport, O.J. (1968) L.175. Also, Regulation 4064/89 on the control of concentrations between undertakings, contains special provisions in respect of credit institutions and other financial institutions, O.J. (1989) L.395.

[49] Case 22/71 *Béguelin Import* [1971] E.C.R. 949.

the fact that, in reality, parent and subsidiary constitute one economic unit.[50] In the *Dyestuffs* case,[51] the Court sought to determine how the various economic units formed one economic entity in order to examine how non-Community undertakings had organised illegal price-fixing within the Community through subsidiaries under their control.

The question of the geographical extent of the Court's jurisdiction in competition cases assumed importance in the interlocutory judgment in a complex case concerning wood pulp,[52] which is still before the Court and where experts' reports on economic and technical questions of detail were sought. In this case a concerted practice was alleged between undertakings in several non-Community countries. The applicants submitted that a decision of the Commission was incompatible with public international law since the Commission had applied competition rules to the economic repercussions within the common market of conduct restricting competition which took place outside the Community. The Advocate General relied, as some of his predecessors had done in other cases, on the "effects" doctrine as applied in the United States; he considered that it was legitimate in the light of international law and of widespread state practice to find the basis of jurisdiction of the Community on the location of direct, substantial and foreseeable effects.[53]

The Court decided the case by reference to conventional international criteria. It ruled that the conclusion

---

[50] Case 6/72 *Continental Can* [1973] E.C.R. 215.

[51] Case 48/69 *Imperial Chemical Industries* [1972] E.C.R. 619.

[52] Joined Cases 89, 104, 114, 116, 117 and 125–129/85 *Åhlström and others* [1988] E.C.R. 5193 (the *Woodpulp* case).

[53] Opinion of Advocate General Darmon in *Woodpulp, supra* at p. 5214. See also Advocate General Mayras in Case 48/69 *ICI, supra*, Advocate General Warner in Joined Cases 6 and 7/73 *Commercial Solvents* [1974] E.C.R. 223, and Advocate General Roemer in Case 6/72 *Continental Can, supra*.

of an agreement "consists of conduct made up of two elements": the making of the agreement and the implementation thereof. If the application of Community law depended on the place where the agreement was made, that would offer an easy means of evading the Treaty provisions on competition. The decisive factor, therefore, is "the place where it is implemented." The Court noted that the producers had implemented their pricing agreement within the Community. "It is immaterial in that respect whether or not they had recourse to subsidiaries, agents, sub-agents, or branches within the Community in order to make their contacts with purchasers within the Community."[54] This was sufficient to establish jurisdiction and the question of whether the Commission was right as to the substance has still to be decided.

How legalistic is the Court when dealing with these cases? How far can it be said to have been "creative"? How conscious is it of procedural rather than substantive law problems?

Legalism or commercial realism?

When the Court has to determine the relevant market in order to decide whether there has been an abuse of a dominant position under Article 86, it uses criteria which are far from being purely legalistic. In the first place it is accepted that goods or services which are interchangeable are part of the same market. This seems a relatively simple criterion but, in practice, the application of this test may prove to be extremely complicated even for humble domestic products. The most striking and well-known example of this is to be found in *United Brands*, where the Court defined the product market in order to

---

[54] *Woodpulp, supra,* p. 5243.

determine whether United Brands held a dominant position on that market. The Court had to decide whether the market in bananas was sufficiently distinct from the markets in other fresh fruit. In the course of its long examination, it ruled that "the banana has certain characteristics, appearance, taste, softness, seedlessness, easy handling, a constant level of production which enable it to satisfy the constant needs of an important section of the population consisting of the very young, the old and the sick."[55]

The Court, in so doing, indicates a method of evaluation but does not substitute its own economic evaluation for the one used by the Commission. Nevertheless, when the relevant market has not been defined with sufficient precision by the Commission, the Court will note the failure and will, if necessary, quash the decision. Not only the characteristics of the product but also the price, its use, and supply and demand are to be taken into account.[56]

Financial and economic considerations arise in some of these cases and cannot be ignored.

How important and difficult the cases can be is shown by the recent decision in *Akzo*[57] where the main issue was price competition and particularly what is known in the United States as predatory pricing. There, the question has been the subject of much debate since 1958[58] but the various criteria suggested by academic

[55] Case 27/76 *United Brands* [1978] E.C.R. 207.

[56] For instance, see Case 322/81 *Michelin* [1983] E.C.R. 3461.

[57] Case C–62/86 *Akzo*, judgment of July 3, 1991, not yet reported, points 71–72.

[58] McGee, Predatory Price Cutting: the Standard Oil (N.J.) Case, J. Law & Econ. 137 (1958). Same author, Predatory Pricing Revisited, J. Law & Econ. 289 (1980). Areeda and Turner, Predatory Pricing and Related Practices under s.2 of the Sherman Act, Harv.L.Rev. 679 (1975). F. M. Scherer, Predatory Pricing and the Sherman Act, Harv.L.Rev. 869 (1976).

writers have yet to find any actual judicial support which might have been helpful to the European Court.

Akzo lodged an application at the Court against a Commission decision of 1985, which found that Akzo had abused its dominant position by taking action against a competing British company (ECS) in a way which was intended to undermine ECS's business and to force it to withdraw from the market in organic peroxides. According to the Commission, Akzo had directly threatened ECS and consistently offered and supplied flour additives to ECS's clients at prices lower than those of ECS. The Commission also criticised Akzo for making selective offers and offers at below cost price; all aimed at undermining other suppliers of flour additives. As a consequence, the Commission imposed a fine of 10 million ECU on Akzo.

For the purpose of deciding if there had been an abuse of a dominant position, the first question was what was the relevant market. The Court held that the Commission was right in taking into account the peroxide market even if Akzo's intention was to undermine its competitor in a different market, that of flour additives, in which market lay ECS's main activity, whereas the peroxide market was the most important for Akzo. Thus, Akzo could practise price-cutting in a market which was vital for ECS but of a limited interest to itself. Akzo could balance its losses on the flour additives market by making profits in the peroxide market by virtue of its monopolistic position.

By fixing "abusively" low prices—prices lower than the average variable costs—the dominant undertaking could thus eliminate its competitor and be able to raise its price again later on the basis of its monopolistic position. That constitutes an abuse of a dominant position. No less, prices lower than the average total costs may be regarded as an abuse of the dominant position where they are fixed as part of a plan to eliminate a competitor; such a practice of price-cutting can remove from the market undertakings which may be as effective as the dominant undertaking but, because of their lesser financial capacity, are unable to resist the competition to which they are subjected.

Creativity

The Court has been called on to decide whether the competition rules apply in particular areas where no specific Community rules have been adopted. Thus, it has ruled that the competition rules may apply to the provision of services, particularly in the banking sector,[59] a decision regarded by banking lawyers as being of much practical importance.

A similar result was achieved in a case concerning air transport.[60] The Treaty leaves it to the Council to decide whether, to what extent, and by what procedure, appropriate provisions should be laid down for sea and air transport.[61] The reluctance of Member States to surrender the regulation of air transport and the fixing of air tariffs, and the existing co-operation on the international level, had delayed Community legislation in this area. Much effort was expended urging the Community legislator to take action, without any success.[62]

The question came before the Court, on a reference under Article 177, in the course of criminal proceedings against the executives of airlines and travel agencies who had been charged with infringement of the French civil aviation code by selling air tickets, in so-called "bucket" shops, priced at tariffs not approved by the French

[59] Case 172/80 *Züchner* [1981] E.C.R. 2021.
[60] Joined Cases 209 to 213/84 *Asjes* [1986] E.C.R. 1425.
[61] Article 84.
[62] See Case 246/81 *Bethell* [1982] E.C.R. 2277.

administration. The Tribunal de Police de Paris asked whether legislation of this kind contravened Community law, in particular Articles 85 and 86 of the Treaty. The Court held that those Articles did apply to air transport even in the absence of a Council decision to that effect.

As a result national authorities and the Commission have the power to apply competition rules in regard to air transport. The Court accepted that it was for Member States to approve air fares. However, where fare levels were set by restrictive agreements or concerted practices, national measures which reinforced the anti-competitive behaviour of the airlines were contrary to Article 85 of the Treaty and a breach of the Member State's obligations. A decision as to whether there had been such an agreement or practice was, however, confined to the designated authorities of the Member States or to the Commission and not merely to the ordinary courts of the Member States.

This judgment added to the pressure on the Community authorities and they have since adopted regulations, a directive and a decision which liberalise air traffic between the Member States and which spell out how far exceptions from the competition rules on restrictive agreements can be granted to airlines companies.[63]

A further striking illustration of the breaking of new ground by the Court, followed by legislation, is to be found in a judgment concerning franchising—*Pronuptia*.[64]

The case involved a dispute over royalty payments between a German subsidiary of Pronuptia (the franchisor) and its German franchisee. The franchise agreement includes, unlike agreements relating to most other

[63] See also Case 66/86 *Ahmed Saeed Flugreisen* [1989] E.C.R. 803.
[64] Case 161/84 *Pronuptia de Paris* v. *Schillgalis* [1986] E.C.R. 353.

distribution systems, a transfer of intellectual property rights—such as the right to use the name, know-how, designs and commercial practices of the franchisor. The system allows a trader, with no experience, rapid access to established commercial practices, and the Court considered it normal that the franchisor should profit from such a system. Accordingly, some clauses of a franchise agreement are both indispensable and justified in order to allow the franchisor to ensure that the franchisees respect common standards and intellectual property rights. On the other hand, some restrictions were not considered essential to the system when they distorted competition by dividing the market territorially between franchisor and franchisees or between individual franchisees or by imposing exclusivity or resale price maintenance clauses.

Following that judgment, the Commission adopted several individual exemption decisions,[65] and then a regulation providing block exemptions,[66] the text of which develops the main thrust of the *Pronuptia* judgment. This case illustrates, as did earlier insurance and air transport decisions, the way in which the Court can lay the foundations of future legislation.

The control of mergers provides another example. In *BAT*,[67] the Court stated, for the first time, that Article 85 could be applied to the acquisition by a company of a minority shareholding in one of its competitors, where that acquisition served as an instrument for influencing the commercial conduct of the companies in question.'' Firstly, the Court encouraged companies to consult the Commission before making such arrangements and,

---

[65] Decisions in Yves Rocher, O.J. (1987) L.8; Computerland, O.J. (1987) L.222; and Service Master, O.J. (1988) L.332.
[66] Regulation No. 4087/88, O.J. (1988) L.359/46.
[67] Joined Cases 142 and 156/84 *British American Tobacco and Reynolds* v. *Commission* [1987] E.C.R. 4487.

secondly, the Court to some extent anticipated the regulation on mergers, which is now in force.

Procedures

In this area, however, it is not just substantive law which counts. In the Community and in the operation of the market, procedural guarantees must be established. For example, the guarantees laid down in Regulation 17/62, which governs the procedures to be followed by the Commission in its investigations, have had to be interpreted. Thus, business secrets must be protected when revealed to the Commission during an investigation,[68] though it is for the Commission, after hearing the parties and subject to review by the Court, to decide whether what is contained in a document constitutes a business secret. Professional secrecy between a client and a lawyer must be respected, though in the leading case, the Court, contrary to the strongly-expressed views of the Advocate General, rejected the contention that there existed a "professional privilege" between client and in-house lawyer or between client and lawyer outside the Community.[69]

In this context, a more recent case[70] dealt with a decision of the Commission concerning search of premises and seizure of documents. The Commission wished, in the course of an investigation, to search the files of some companies, especially those of Hoechst A.G. Hoechst refused the Commission access, alleging that it was an illegal search, violating fundamental rights granted by Community law. Although Regulation 17

[68] Case 53/85 *Akzo Chemie BV* [1986] E.C.R. 1965.
[69] Case 155/79 *AM & S Europe* v. *Commission* [1982] E.C.R. 1575. See, however, Case T–30/89 *Hilti* v. *Commission* [1990] E.C.R. II–163.
[70] Joined Cases 46/87 and 227/88 *Hoechst* v. *Commission* [1989] E.C.R. 2919.

permits such a search, it would, Hoechst argued, still be contrary to the rights of the defence and would be an invasion of the company's privacy unless it were authorised by proper judicial procedures. The Court, in its judgment, reiterated the necessity to protect both fundamental rights and the rights of defendants including protection of the premises of undertakings. However, the Court emphasised that all the judicial systems of the Member States provide protection against arbitrary and disproportionate interventions by public bodies. The Court concluded, therefore, that although there is no general principle of law which grants immunity to business premises, Regulation 17 requires the Commission to follow the procedures laid down by national law, whether administrative or judicial, when entering and searching business premises.

The right to a fair hearing was again raised, one month later, in *Orkem* and *Solvay*.[71] The Court held that there is no rule of privilege against self-incrimination in the course of a preliminary investigation, either on the basis of the rules relevant in criminal law or on the basis of the European Convention of Human Rights. The right to a fair hearing should not, however, be imperilled at any stage of a procedure and the company under investigation cannot be compelled to answer questions requiring it to admit a breach of Articles 85 or 86.

Limitations are thus placed on the Commission's powers because of the need to safeguard the rights of the defence, which right the Court has held to be a fundamental principle of Community law.[72] This is not a purely legalistic concern. The creation of a single market through the development of trade depends very much

---

[71] Case 374/87 *Orkem* v. *Commission* [1989] E.C.R. 3283; Case 27/88 *Solvay* v. *Commission* [1989] E.C.R. 3355.
[72] Case 322/82 *Michelin* v. *Commission* [1983] E.C.R. 3461.

upon the free development of undertakings. They must, therefore, be afforded the right to explain and defend the position which they take.

C. THE COMMON MARKET AND INTERNATIONAL TRADE

The creation of the common market and the emphasis on the freedom of movement of goods as the very foundation of the Community, does not mean that the Community is not concerned with the rest of the world. There are important provisions of the Treaty dealing with the external relations and policies of the Community which have given rise to important judgments by the Court, so much so that Judge Pescatore wrote, even ten years ago, that it was the Court which had delineated the international profile of the Community.[73]

This results, in part, from the fact that the Community is a customs union with a common customs tariff applicable to non-Member States; in part, because the Community is committed to contributing to the harmonious development of world trade and the progressive abolition of restrictions on international trade[74]; in part, because the Community is to have a common commercial policy based on "uniform principles particularly in regard to changes in tariff rates, the conclusion of tariff and trade agreements, the achievement of uniformity in measures of liberalisation."[75] In addition, the Court has jurisdiction to give an opinion, at

[73] P. Pescatore, "Aspects judiciaires de l'acquis communautaire", *Revue trimestrielle de droit européen*, (1981), p. 636.
[74] Article 110.
[75] Article 113.

the request of the Council, the Commission or a Member State, on the compatibility of a proposed agreement between the Community and one or more states or an international organisation. Such an opinion has recently been sought in respect of the proposed agreement with the EFTA countries.[76] If the Court rules that the proposed agreement is not compatible with the Treaty, then the Treaty must be amended by the unanimous agreement of, and ratification by, all the Member States to make it possible.[77]

It was inevitable, even allowing for a large measure of discretion on the part of those institutions when defining and applying the relevant principles and policies in the field of international trade, that the Court should be asked to decide whether the measures adopted by the Council and the Commission were compatible with the Treaty. For example, the Court has ruled that, where the Council has adopted a general regulation in order to implement one of the objectives laid down in Article 113, it cannot derogate from those rules when dealing with a specific case.[78]

It is clear however that the Court is reluctant to uphold arguments which could mean interference with major aspects of, and changes in, policy. For instance, in cases concerning imports of preserved mushrooms from Taiwan, after the signing of a trade agreement between the Community and the People's Republic of China, the Court stated that "Community institutions enjoy discretion in the sphere of commercial policy"[79] and it rejected the argument that the measures introduced by the Commission were disproportionate.

[76] Opinion C–1/91.
[77] Article 236.
[78] Cases 113/77 *NTN Toyo Bearing Co. Ltd.* [1979] E.C.R. 1185 *et seq.*
[79] Case 245/81 *Edeka* [1982] E.C.R. 2745.

"In view of the fact that the Commission sought by means of the contested measures to achieve two equally legitimate objectives, namely stabilisation of the market and implementation of a Community policy relating to external trade, the measures adopted cannot be considered to be disproportionate to the objectives pursued. It is an unavoidable fact that changes in Community policies relating to external trade have repercussions on the prospects of traders in the sector concerned."[80]

The common customs tariff fixes duties for every product which enters the Community from a third country. Obviously, if the common market is to mean anything, the duties must be identical regardless of whichever Member State the product first enters. The nomenclature is increasingly complex and the Court has been called on to decide a body of cases of considerable commercial importance, if sometimes not of great legal difficulty, which are aimed at eliminating divergent interpretations by national administrations. The Court has frequently underlined the fact that the common customs tariff is intended to achieve an equalisation of customs charges levied at the frontiers of the Community on products imported from third countries in order to avoid any deflection of trade with those countries and any distortion of free internal circulation or of competitive conditions.

Because of this need to achieve uniformity, the Court ruled that Member States may not unilaterally fix new charges or alter the level of existing charges whether or not the duties are protective in nature. This is a matter now for the institutions of the Community.[81]

---

[80] Case 52/81 *Faust* [1982] E.C.R. 3745.
[81] Joined Cases 37 and 38/73 *Diamantarbeiders* v. *Indiamex* [1973] E.C.R. 1609.

Normally, the Court will explain the basis on which one of the headings is to be applied, or will define objective criteria to be applied, leaving it to the authorities to take the final decision. Occasionally, however, it is virtually impossible to define the criteria without deciding whether the object is or is not within a given tariff heading.[82]

Sometimes the Court moves outside the field of ordinary commerce. Thus the question was posed, on a reference by a national court, as to whether an object—a wall relief made of cardboard and expanded polystyrene, sprayed with black paint and oil, and attached to a wooden panel by means of wire and synthetic resin—should be regarded as a work of art.[83]

Procedurally more difficult have been the cases where the question has arisen as to whether, under the Community regulations implementing the Florence Agreement drawn up under the auspices of UNESCO, scientific apparatus can be imported by universities free of duties and charges if they are for educational purposes or scientific research. This is largely a matter for the national authorities, the Commission and a group of experts representing the Member States. The Court does not itself decide whether the apparatus is of a scientific nature or whether the equivalent equipment is available in the Community, but it does decide whether, on the face of the decision, the criteria adopted by the Commission took account of the objective characteristics of the product.[84]

---

[82] Case 245/87 *Blaupunkt-Werke GmbH* [1989] E.C.R. 573 (summary publication).

[83] Case 155/84 *Onnasch* [1985] E.C.R. 1449.

[84] Case 294/81 *Control Data Belgium* [1983] E.C.R. 911. See also Case C–269/90 *Technische Universität München*, judgment of November 21, 1991, not yet reported.

As part of the common commercial policy, the Community has adopted measures concerning protection against dumping and the origin of goods. Rules relating to exports and imports and to credit insurance have been made, either for specific goods such as textiles, or for particular groups of countries such as the (former) state-trading countries of Central and Eastern Europe. The Court, under its supervisory jurisdiction, is called upon to ensure that these rules are made under the appropriate article of the Treaty, which my affect the question whether the decision is to be unanimous or by a majority. It may have to decide questions of procedure, or as to whether a particular type of importer or exporter has *locus standi* to challenge anti-dumping duties. Its rulings are not infrequently sought by exporters wishing to have set aside findings of dumping or as to the margin of dumping or of injury to the Community. These cases can be very complex in their detail, involve vast documentation, substantial sums of money and sometimes, it must be said, very ingenious arguments. I have heard Japanese lawyers and businessmen criticising the Court for failing to take a more active part in the factual appraisal or the economic appreciation. This, however, is to misunderstand the process of judicial review and it is not a criticism to say that the Court is cautious in interfering in complex economic situations or in reviewing the calculation of anti-dumping duties.

There have, however, been two areas of broader principle where the Court has had to take major decisions.

1. THE COMMUNITY AND INTERNATIONAL AGREEMENTS

The first involves the power of the Community to enter into international agreements which might, after a first glance at Article 228, appear somewhat limited. Thus, the Commission is to negotiate agreements "where the Treaty provides for the conclusion" of such agreements. This might be taken to mean that the Community's treaty-making powers depend upon specific articles such as Article 113 on the common commercial policy or those in relation to international organisations[85] or association agreements with other states.[86]

The Court, however, early developed a theory of implied powers in relation to the Community's competence—powers are said to arise not only from the provisions giving express authority to enter into agreements but also, by implication, from other provisions granting the Community power to act internally and even from action undertaken in the application of such provisions by the Council and the Commission. This has not only a positive side, in favour of the Community, but a negative side in that it limits the powers of the Member States. Thus, in *ERTA*,[87] the Court stated that:

> "each time the Community, with a view to implementing a common policy envisaged by the Treaty, adopts provisions laying down common rules, whatever form these may take, the Member States no longer have the right, acting individually or even collectively, to undertake obligations with third countries which affect those rules."

In later cases the Court confirmed those implied powers of the Community and particularly in its Opinion, given in 1977, on the validity of a draft agreement on a

---

[85] Articles 229 to 231.
[86] Article 238.
[87] Case 22/70 *Commission* v. *Council* [1971] E.C.R. 263.

European laying-up fund for inland waterway vessels.[88] As a result, the Community is empowered to conclude agreements in all those fields—such as fisheries, transport, energy—where the Community has adopted measures applicable in the Community. However, as long as the Community has not exercised its power in those fields, the Member States retain jurisdiction to conclude agreements.[89]

On the other hand, in the commercial policy area, the Community has an exclusive jurisdiction to enter into agreements, whether or not there are internal rules on the matter.[90] Moreover, although Member States have lost the power to conclude such agreements, they retain both powers and obligations relating to the carrying out of such agreements on their territories.[91]

Agreements entered into by the Community are as acts of "one of the institutions of the Community within the meaning of Article 177" and, as from their entry into force, the provisions of such agreements "form an integral part of the Community legal system." So, the Court has jurisdiction to give preliminary rulings concerning the interpretation of such agreements.[92]

For some agreements, the Court may be faced with major political issues which go beyond purely commercial considerations.

In *Bulk Oil*, the issue concerned quantitative restrictions imposed in 1979 by the United Kingdom on exports of crude oil to some non-Member countries, in particular Israel. This policy was not incorporated in legislation or in a ministerial order—it was not strictly a "ban"—but

---

[88] Opinion 1/76 [1977] E.C.R. 741; also Joined Cases 3, 4 and 6/76 *Kramer* [1976] E.C.R. 1279.

[89] *Kramer, supra;* Case 61/77 *Commission* v. *Ireland* [1978] E.C.R. 417.

[90] Opinion 1/75 [1975] E.C.R. 1355 and Opinion 1/78 [1979] E.C.R. 2871.

[91] Case 12/86 *Demirel* [1987] E.C.R. 3719.

[92] Case 181/73 *Haegeman* [1974] E.C.R. 449; Case 12/86 *Demirel, supra.*

the firm attitude of the British Government appears to have been an effective deterrent as British Petroleum refused to supply oil to a purchaser when it discovered that the final destination was Israel.[93] The Court had to assess the validity of the restrictions under the common commercial policy and under the EEC-Israel agreement. The Court did not find that the agreement, or the regulation establishing common rules for exports, prohibited Member States from imposing new quantitative restrictions or measures having equivalent effect on exports of oil to non-Member countries. It held that Article 113 did not prevent the Council, in the exercise of the discretion which it enjoys in economic matters of such complexity, from excluding certain products from the common rules on exports. It appeared to the Court that such an exclusion was permissible in the case of oil, "in view of international commitments entered into by certain Member States and taking into account the particular characteristics of that product, which is of vital importance for the economy of a State and for the functioning of its institutions and public services."

2. THE GENERAL AGREEMENT ON TARIFFS AND TRADE

The second area of importance involves specifically the GATT.

In the leading case, which recognised international law as binding on the Communities, the GATT was the specific convention referred to.[94] Although the Community is not a signatory to the GATT, as an

---

[93] Case 174/84 *Bulk Oil* v. *Sun International* [1986] E.C.R. 559. See also Case 14/74 *Norddeutsches Vieh und Fleischkontor* [1974] E.C.R. 899 and Case 23/79 *Geflügelschlachterei Freystadt* [1979] E.C.R. 2789.

[94] Joined Cases 21–24/72 *International Fruit Company* [1972] E.C.R. 1219.

international body it has become effectively a contracting party though the practice under international common law. Thus, it has been entitled to negotiate in the various "Rounds"—Kennedy, Tokyo, Uruguay—and the Court has stated that "since so far as fulfilment of the commitments provided for by GATT is concerned, the Community has replaced the Member States, the mandatory effect, in law, of these commitments must be determined by reference to the relevant provisions in the Community legal system and not to those which gave them their previous force under national legal systems."[95]

As a result of this substitution of the Community for the Member States, the provisions of the GATT are among those on which the Court of Justice has jurisdiction to give preliminary rulings under Article 177—"even where the national court is requested to apply them with reference to relations between individuals for purposes other than that of determining whether a Community measure is valid"—as the Court ruled in *Michelin Italiana*.[96]

Nevertheless, this has not so far given rise to the direct effect of GATT in the Community. In *International Fruit*,[97] the Court denied direct effect to this agreement, after consideration of "the spirit, general scheme and terms" of the GATT. The Court based that decision on two main arguments. Firstly, it held that the agreement is founded on the principle of negotiations undertaken on the basis of "reciprocal and mutually advantageous arrangements." Secondly, the agreement is characterised by the great flexibility of its provisions; this is exemplified by the possibility of derogation, the measures to be applied in cases of exceptional difficulties and,

---

[95] Case 38/75 *Nederlandse Spoorwegen* [1975] E.C.R. 1439.
[96] Joined Cases 267–269/81 *SPI and SAMI* [1983] E.C.R. 801.
[97] Joined Cases 21–24/72, *supra.*

more particularly, the settlement of conflicts between the contracting parties.

This judgment, later confirmed in other cases, has been much criticised.

Whether this decision applies to all GATT provisions may still be open to debate. There are those who strongly believe that GATT is too much of a reciprocal trade-off and too discretionary for it to be directly enforceable in the national courts. On the other hand, the provisions of some international agreements have been recognised as having direct effect, even though they result from negotiations with specific countries, such as the Yaoundé Convention, the association agreement with Greece and the agreement with Portugal.[98] For the Court,

> "a provision in an agreement must be regarded as being directly applicable when, regard being had to its wording and the purpose and nature of the agreement itself, the provision contains a clear and precise obligation which is not subject, in its implementation or effects, to the adoption of any subsequent measure."[99]

Moreover, the existence of institutions set up by agreement, such as a mechanism for dispute settlement, does not constitute a definite hindrance to direct effect. In *Kupferberg*,[1] the Court ruled that:

> "The mere fact that the contracting parties have established a special institutional framework for consultations and negotiations *inter se* in relation to the

[98] Case 87/75 *Bresciani* [1976] E.C.R. 129, Case 17/81 *Pabst und Richarz* [1982] E.C.R. 1331 and Case 104/81 *Kupferberg* [1982] E.C.R. 3641.
[99] Case 12/86 *Demirel, supra.*
[1] Case 104/81, *supra.*

implementation of the agreement is not in itself sufficient to exclude all judicial application of that agreement."

As long as GATT is part of the Community legal order, judicial review of Community acts is possible on the basis of an infringement of the agreement itself, or of an agreement concluded by the Community within the GATT framework.

It has been suggested that judicial review should be based solely on Community law,[2] and that the Court would be reluctant to substitute its own interpretation of the GATT for that of the GATT institutions. However, since the Court has held that GATT obligations are binding on the Community, it is clear that applicants may invoke GATT rules. This they do, especially in actions brought against Community regulations imposing anti-dumping duties. Since those regulations were adopted on the basis of the basic Community anti-dumping regulations of 1979, 1984 and 1988, which are in turn based on the GATT[3] anti-dumping code, the parties tend increasingly to invoke GATT rules.[4]

This may raise difficulties for the Court in some cases. It is not for the European Court to give an authoritative interpretation of GATT law on a world scale. But the Court cannot avoid ensuring a uniform interpretation

---

[2] Advocate General Roemer in Joined Cases 41–44/70 *International Fruit Company* [1971] E.C.R. 436.

[3] For instance, in Joined Cases C–133 and C–150/87 *Nashua* and Case C–156/87 *Gestetner Holdings* ([1990] E.C.R. I – 719 and I – 781 respectively), the Court pointed out that the Commission's practice of not accepting undertakings from importers is based in particular on the GATT anti-dumping code.

[4] Case 240/84 *NTN Toyo Bearing* [1987] E.C.R. 1809, Case 255/84 *Nachi Fujikoshi* [1987] E.C.R. 1861, Case 256/84 *Koyo Seiko* [1987] E.C.R. 1899, Case 260/84 *Minebea* [1987] E.C.R. 1975.

and application of the GATT in the Community legal system. The fundamental justification for that lies in the need for the unity of the Community. The Court has made this clear, holding that "any difference in the interpretation and application of provisions binding the Community as regards non-Member countries would not only jeopardise the unity of the commercial policy, which according to Article 113 of the Treaty must be based on uniform principles, but also create distortions in trade within the Community as a result of the differences in the manner in which the agreement in force between the Community and non-Member countries were applied in the various Member States."[5]

Thus, if the Court has been expansive in relation to the Community's powers to make agreements, it has so far taken a restrictive stand in relation to the application of GATT which may, in view of the issues currently been raised, and likely to be raised in the future, become of increasing importance.

Conclusion

These examples—and they are only illustrations—show how important has been the participation of the Court in bringing the market into being and making it effective. The free movement of goods is the starting point but the ancillary policies and the role of the Community in world trade are inseparably linked to the overriding aims. No less important is the development of rules affecting those who live and work in the Community.

---

[5] Joined Cases 267–169/81, *supra* at 828.

3. AFFECTING THE PEOPLE

It is plain that many of the steps taken to bring about a common market or a single market will have an effect on the lives of people. Sometimes this will be direct, sometimes it is less direct.

If technical, fiscal and physical barriers to trade are removed, goods should be available more readily in all the Member States. There should be a greater variety of supply. Goods should be delivered more quickly. In the end, goods should be available more cheaply to the consumer.

When discriminatory taxation was removed, the Italian purchaser could get his whisky cheaper. Wine duties in the United Kingdom had to be changed to equate with those imposed on beer and whisky. The consumer gets his product more cheaply. On the other hand, if anti-dumping duties are imposed, industry in the Community will be protected, but it may be that, as a result of the reaction of importers, wholesalers and retailers, the consumer will have to pay more. If State aids are forbidden, some industries may go to the wall so that there is unemployment. Yet overall, ensuring free competition in the Community should, in the long term, be of direct advantage to the consumer.

There are, however, other ways in which the individual is, or may be, more directly affected by Community policies and by the judgments of the Court of Justice. It is these that I consider in this lecture. If there is to be a common market or a single market then it is clear that not only goods but also people should have rights to move around for broadly economic purposes. It may be that eventually there will be a right for everybody to move around the Community freely, for whatever reason and in whatever context, subject to such restrictions as are justified by the protection of public security and public order. Perhaps it is not only that there "will be," but that under the Treaty there "should be," such a right since it is to be remembered that one of the "activities" of the Community, expressed in Article 3(1) of the Treaty, is to be the abolition as between Member States of obstacles to freedom of movement for persons. We are not at that stage yet. There have, however, been developments of considerable importance which either have affected, or are likely to affect, the extent to which the citizens of the Member States can move around inside the European Community.

WORKERS

I begin with "workers," numerically the largest and economically the most relevant group in the context of the European Economic Treaty.

Free movement

By Article 48 of the Treaty, freedom of movement for workers was to be secured within the Community by the end of the transitional period at the latest, that is to say by December 31, 1969. "Freedom of movement for workers" requires the abolition of any discrimination based on nationality between workers of the Member States as regards employment, remuneration and other conditions of work and employment. This freedom is said to entail the right to accept offers of employment; to move freely within the territories of the Member States and to stay in a Member State for this purpose; and to remain there after having been employed in that State.

Inevitably, the realisation of this right required detailed legislation and the Council was given power, on a proposal from the Commission and in co-operation with the Parliament, to issue directives or to make regulations setting out the measures required. These were intended, in particular, to ensure close co-operation between national employment services, to abolish systematically and progressively practices which formed an obstacle to the free movement of workers and which imposed conditions regarding the free choice of employment applicable to workers other than those of the State concerned.

The Council has issued directives and made regulations to achieve these purposes.[1] However, these provisions are, although very important, only the starting point and the Court has been called on to play an important role in their further definition.

Article 48, at first glance, may seem very straightforward. It gives rights to "workers"; in particular rights to accept offers of employment actually made. However, a

[1] Council Regulation 1612/68/EEC of October 15, 1968, on freedom of movement of workers, (O.J. English Special Edition, 1968) (II), p. 475. Council Directive 68/360/EEC of October 15, 1968, on the abolition of restrictions on movement and residence within the Community for workers of Member States and their families, (O.J. English Special Edition, 1968) (II), p. 485.

number of questions arise. What is a "worker?" If a man or a woman has not actually been offered a job but wants to go to look for work—does he have any rights under an article which provides that he may "accept offers of employment actually made?" What are the rights of his family if he has a right to move about? What is the influence on his social security rights if he does move around the Community? What rights, if any, does he have against his own Member State under this Article and the legislation made under it?

"Worker" is not defined and it is often words, the meaning of which is taken for granted, which give the greatest difficulty. As a starting point it was quite clear that "worker" had to be given the same meaning throughout the Community. Somebody who is a worker in one country could not be allowed to be treated as not being a worker in another for the purposes of rights conferred by this Article. It was, therefore, for the Court to lay down Community definitions of "worker" and "activity as an employed person" which were applicable throughout the Community for the purposes of Article 48, though not necessarily for other purposes. National judges, therefore, had to adopt a Community law definition for these purposes even if the definition was different from that applicable in their national legal systems.

In language not unfamiliar to an English lawyer, the Court has laid down that "the essential feature of an employment relationship is that for a certain period of time a person performs services for and under the direction of another person in return for which he receives remuneration."[2] There must thus be a link of subordination and the undertaking of a task in return for remuneration.

---

[2] Case 66/85 *Lawrie-Blum* [1986] E.C.R. 2121.

The application of this definition to the man or woman who works regularly 40 hours a week for a salary is obviously not very difficult. In the present climate, however, not everyone is able to, nor wishes to, fit into this simple pattern. People work in different ways for different periods and subject to different conditions and from time to time it is necessary to consider whether they can be described as "workers" who are entitled to these rights. The concept of worker has to be considered in the light of the nature of the rights conferred and Member States are clearly very much concerned to know who has the right to move freely within the territory of a Member State and to stay there. They are no'less concerned to know whether the rights conferred by the Community's legislation on workers applies to everyone who has undoubtedly done some work.

It was inevitable that the question would arise in relation to part-time workers. Are all part-time workers "workers" for the purposes of Article 48 or are there limits? Mrs. Levin, who is a British citizen, claimed that she was entitled to reside in the Netherlands and to have her South African husband with her, on the ground that she was a worker. The Dutch authorities took the view that she was not engaged in a gainful occupation and was not a worker for the purposes of Article 48 because she had accepted a part-time job as a maid in an hotel simply in order to enable her husband to come in. Moreover, she did not earn the minimum wage considered necessary in the Netherlands for an acceptable standard of living. Nor did she work a fixed minimum number of hours. The question was, therefore, whether in order to be a worker and to have the rights conferred by Article 48 and by the regulation, a person had to work a minimum number of hours and obtain a minimum remuneration, in this particular case the subsistence wage recognised by Dutch law.

The Court rejected the argument that she could not be a worker unless she earned a minimum subsistence wage and unless she did a minimum number of hours for the purposes of the Dutch legislation. This is not required either by the Treaty or by the appropriate regulation and directive. The Court had no doubt that the concept of "worker" and "activity as an employed person" concerned also "persons who pursue or wish to pursue an activity as an employed person on a part-time basis and who, by virtue of that fact, obtain or would obtain only remuneration lower than the minimum guaranteed remuneration in the sector under consideration." What mattered was that the job should be effective and genuine employment even if it were part-time.[3]

In that case the persons involved had some income and some private means which enabled them to survive without substantial income from employment. It was not difficult to see that a question would arise where someone had no income or private means.

The case which followed involved a German national, also working in the Netherlands, as a part-time music teacher.[4] He did not have private means but received supplementary benefits out of public funds in accordance with Dutch national rules on unemployment benefit, social assistance and sickness insurance. He too was refused a residence permit and a question was eventually referred to the European Court. The argument put to us was that, even if a part-time worker with private means could be regarded as a "worker," it was quite wrong that a person dependent on social security should be regarded as a worker. This argument, which had a mid-nineteenth century ring about it, was perhaps

[3] Case 53/81 *Levin* [1982] E.C.R. 1035.
[4] Case 139/85 *Kempf* [1986] E.C.R. 1741.

sociologically somewhat surprising and the Court had no difficulty in rejecting it. It was held that

> "it is irrelevant whether those supplementary means of subsistence are derived from property or from the employment of a member of his family, as was the case in *Levin*, or whether, as in this instance, they are obtained from financial assistance drawn from the public funds of the Member State in which he resides, provided that the effective and genuine nature of his work is established."

The right which is conferred is obviously intended to enable workers to move from one Member State to another. A worker who has always lived and worked in his own Member State cannot, however, rely on Article 48 of the Treaty to establish Community rights against that Member State and thereby override national legislation. Thus, a German national, who was denied access to a teacher training course because of his membership of the Communist Party, argued that the refusal to allow him to qualify in Germany made it impossible for him to apply for teaching posts in schools in other Member States. This, he said, was a restriction on his rights of free movement. The Court however, whilst underlining that freedom of movement does not apply to situations which are wholly internal to a Member State, commented: "A purely hypothetical prospect of employment in another Member State does not establish a sufficient connection with Community law to justify the application of Article 48 of the Treaty."[5]

On the other hand, where a worker has moved out of his own Member State and acquired a qualification in

---

[5] Case 180/83 *Moser* [1984] E.C.R. 2539.

another Member State, he may, on returning to his own country to work, be entitled to invoke Community law against the authorities of his own State.[6]

Once a worker has exercised his Community law right of free movement so that he is entitled to the benefit of the regulations made under Article 49, a question may arise as to his legal position if he then leaves his host Member State on a temporary basis. In one case,[7] a Belgian national was employed by a French company which placed its workers temporarily at the disposal of other undertakings. He was sent to work in Nigeria on a temporary basis. The local sickness insurance fund in Paris refused to regard him as covered by the French social security scheme while he was in Nigeria. The Court held that the insurance fund was wrong to take this view. The worker had established his rights in France and

> "activities temporarily carried on outside the territory of the Community are not sufficient to exclude the application of that principle [*i.e.* of non-discrimination], as long as the employment relationship retains a sufficiently close link with that territory."

The Court has been very firm in insisting on the right of free movement as a basic foundation of the Community. Its attitude can be illustrated in a number of ways. Thus, in the first place, it would seem on the face of it that Article 48, which confers a right to accept an offer of employment, to move about for that purpose, to stay in order to work, and even to stay after the work is finished, does, in express terms, not give any right to

[6] Case 115/78 *Knoors* [1979] E.C.R. 399.
[7] Case 237/83 *Prodest* [1984] E.C.R. 3153.

travel to another Member State in order to look for employment. The Court has, however, held that the right "to enter the territory of another Member State and reside there for the purposes intended by the Treaty, in particular to look for or pursue an occupation ... , is a right conferred directly by the Treaty."[8] This may seem a very desirable result seen from the point of view of the worker but I confess that I had great difficulty in accepting that this flowed from the wording of Article 48 itself. Moreover, it seems somewhat inconsistent with the Court's view that a purely hypothetical prospect of employment in another Member State does not establish a sufficient connection with Community law. However, the point now seems well established. The justification for the ruling that the worker is to be regarded as having a right to go to look for work is clearly that, if such a right were not recognised, then freedom of movement would, for a large number of people, be illusory.

On the other hand, there must be some limits to this right of movement for the purposes of Article 48. How long can a man or woman be said to be looking for employment so as to claim his rights?

The Council, at the time it adopted Regulation 1612/68 and Directive 68/360, declared that nationals of one Member State who move to another Member State in order to seek work, should be allowed a minimum of three months for that purpose. If they had not found employment by the end of the period, their residence in the territory of the second Member State could be brought to an end.

The United Kingdom was more generous. It allowed a period of six months before someone claiming to be

---

[8] Case 48/75 *Royer* [1976] E.C.R. 497.

looking for work was required to leave. In a recent case,[9] the man involved claimed that this was a restriction on his rights and that it was not lawful to lay down any minimum period as long as he was looking for work. It was argued that either you are looking for work or you are not looking for work. If you are looking for work then no limitation is justified. The case provoked very strong arguments on both sides but the Court accepted that, in the absence of a Community provision prescribing the period during which Community nationals may seek employment in a Member State other than their own, a period of six months, as laid down in the United Kingdom, was not in principle insufficient to enable the person concerned to explore the availability of employment. Such a limitation does not jeopardise the effectiveness of the principle of free movement. However, the Court added that "if after the expiry of that period the person concerned provides evidence that he is continuing to seek employment and that he has genuine chances of being engaged, he cannot be required to leave the territory of the host Member State."

Just as the Court has been liberal in interpreting the rights conferred by Article 48 and the subordinate legislation made in connection with those rights, so equally it has been astute to strike down practices which might amount to a technical interference with the exercise of the right of movement by Community nationals. These cases are not confined to workers. They concern all those who have rights of movement. Once a right to enter or reside is established under the Treaty then the general principle has been applied that Member States may not impose administrative restrictions on that right. Thus, in the present context, a worker can enter a

[9] Case C–292/89 *Antonissen*, judgment of February 26, 1991, not yet reported.

Member State simply on production of a valid identity card. Once he shows that he is a worker and either has an offer of employment which he has accepted or is looking for work then he has a right under the Treaty to enter and reside.

The grant of a residence permit is not in itself the basis of his rights: they come from the Treaty itself. On the other hand, some administrative practices of control may be acceptable provided that they do not interfere with the effective exercise of the right. Thus, a Member State may require nationals of other Member States to report their presence to the authorities of that State as long as such a formality does not restrict freedom of movement or limit the right of entry and residence.[10] However a formal grant of leave to enter is neither necessary nor justified.[11] On the other hand, if the time allowed for making a declaration of arrival is not reasonable or there are penalties for failure to discharge the obligation which are disproportionate, these may amount to an unjustified restriction which the Court will strike down. Thus in a very recent case, the Court has ruled that it is incompatible with Community law "to impose on nationals of other Member States exercising their right to freedom of movement the obligation, subject to a penal sanction for failure to comply, to make a declaration of residence within three days of entering" the territory of a Member State.[12]

Achieving a balance between the exercise of the right of freedom of movement and the need for a Member State to be satisfied that the right exists, is not easy. How far can a Member State go in checking at the frontier whether a person has a right of residence? This

[10] Case 118/75 *Watson and Belmann* [1976] E.C.R. 1185.
[11] Case 157/79 *Pieck* [1980] E.C.R. 2171.
[12] Case C–265/88 *Lothar Messner* [1989] E.C.R. 4209.

question arose in an acute form in a recent case involving the Netherlands.[13] Community nationals entering the Netherlands were subject to certain controls and could be questioned about the purpose and duration of their journey and the financial means at their disposal for the purposes of that journey, before they were permitted to enter the territory of the Netherlands. It was strongly argued that since the Member State was only required to let in persons who had a right of residence, the Member State was entitled to carry out random checks at the frontiers to see whether such right of residence existed. The Court rejected this argument and held that by maintaining in force and applying legislation which required nationals of other Member States to answer such questions the Netherlands was in breach of the Treaty.

This decision, of course, applies not only to workers but also to those seeking to establish a business or profession or to provide and obtain the benefit of services in another Member State. Since it has been held that Community nationals have a right to go into other Member States to receive services, which can include medical treatment, education, and tourist facilities,[14] the decision was far-reaching. In my view it was not self-evident. It seems to me clear that Member States must be able to check that persons coming in do not constitute a security risk. It may thus be necessary, if someone says he is a tourist, to ensure that he has the money to stay as a tourist. That is the only right upon which he can rely. Moreover, the Court has accepted that the document presented to justify entry must be a valid document.[15] Therefore, it must be possible for the

---

[13] Case C–68/89 *Commission* v. *Netherlands*, judgment of May 30, 1991, not yet reported.

[14] Joined Cases 266/82 and 26/83 *Luisi and Carbone* [1984] E.C.R. 377.

[15] Case 69/89 *Commission* v. *Netherlands*, *supra*.

authorities at the point of entry to ascertain that the document is a valid passport or identity card. It seems to me also that in the present fight against drugs it is reasonable that a Member State should have the right to ask questions to ascertain whether the person entering is in fact carrying drugs. It may be that if a person enters a country insisting that he is to stay as a tourist for some weeks but he has no money, this could indicate that he is carrying drugs which he will sell in order to maintain himself. It does not, of course, follow from the fact that he has no money that he is carrying drugs but it is a possibility which it seems to me, Member States are entitled to investigate. The Court, however, has rejected this argument as a basis for general questioning.

The worker's family

The right of free movement would be illusory if a worker could not take his spouse, his children and perhaps other members of his family with him. Accordingly, extensive provisions[16] have been adopted to confer rights on members of the family and these rights, unlike those of the worker himself, extend to nationals of non-Member States, and questions frequently arise as to the extent of their rights. The Court has again taken a liberal view of these provisions. Thus, it is accepted that a member of the family may acquire rights of residence even if that member does not live permanently with the worker. A national of Senegal, married to a French worker employed in Berlin, worked in the same city. After she and her husband were separated, she decided to continue to live in Berlin. However, when her residence permit expired she could

[16] See note 1.

not get it renewed because she no longer shared a common domicile with her husband. The Court accepted that as long as they were married, even though they were not living permanently together, she had a right of residence.[17]

Similarly, in a striking case, a question arose as to whether the British companion of an unmarried British worker employed in the Netherlands could claim to be entitled to reside in the Netherlands under Community law.[18] The worker had taken up a temporary post with a subsidiary of a British undertaking in the Netherlands. He had had a stable relationship for five years with his companion but they were not married. It was argued that she should be treated as his spouse for the purposes of Community legislation. The Court rejected this argument on the basis that "spouse" in family law included only someone who enjoyed rights and obligations within a marital relationship. The woman was, therefore, not a spouse. However, the Court pointed out that, under the 1968 Council regulation, a worker who is a national of another Member State must "enjoy the same social and tax advantages as national workers" in the host State. "Social advantages" was not a phrase to be interpreted restrictively. Accordingly, the possibility for a migrant worker to obtain permission for his companion to reside with him, where that companion is also a migrant, "can assist his integration in the host State and thus contribute to the achievement of freedom of movement for workers." Since the Netherlands granted social advantages to its own nationals living together in this way it could not refuse such advantages to workers who were nationals of other Member States without being guilty of discrimination.

[17] Case 267/83 *Diatta* [1986] E.C.R. 567.
[18] Case 59/85 *Reed* [1986] E.C.R. 1283.

Once again, however, the rights are to be accorded only in a Community context. Thus a worker, employed in his own country, who has not exercised a Community law right as a worker to move, cannot claim, under Community law, to bring in his parents, who are not nationals of his Member State. That is entirely a matter of national law and has nothing to do with Community rules at present.[19] It may seem a little curious that a national of one Member State can bring in his family if he has moved to another State as a worker, yet a citizen of that other State, whose parents are not nationals of that State, would have no such right to come in. However strange it may seem at first sight, the distinction is well founded. It is only in a situation where Community rights have been exercised by the worker that he can claim the extended rights for his family. If he has not exercised a Community right then the whole matter has to be dealt with under national law. It is for national law to decide whether the members of the family who are not nationals have such rights.

Suppose that a Community national, whose spouse is not a Community national, goes to another Member State to work and then returns to her own State. Does the spouse have a right to stay in that Member State? That is the question raised in a case which is presently before the Court.[20]

The Treaty makes it clear that a worker has a right of residence after he has retired. By a 1970 Council regulation,[21] the Community recognised the right of survivors of a deceased worker to remain in the Member

[19] Joined Cases 35 and 36/82 *Morson and Jhanjan* [1982] E.C.R. 3723.

[20] Case C–370/90 *Immigration Appeal Tribunal* v. *Mr. S. Singh*, pending.

[21] Regulation 1251/70 on the right of workers to remain in the territory of a Member State after having been employed in that State, (O.J. English Special Edition, 1970), p. 402.

State where the worker resided. They are entitled to social and tax advantages from which the survivors of a national worker would also benefit. Moreover, a right of residence has recently been granted to employees and self-employed persons who have ceased their occupational activity.[22] That right does not depend on the worker having exercised the right to move for the purposes of working during his working life. It is an additional right granted to nationals of Member States who have pursued an activity as an employee or as a self-employed person, and to members of their families, provided that their resources are sufficient to live in the host State and provided that they are covered by sickness insurance in respect of medical risks in the host Member State.

Thus, it is clear that so far as workers are concerned, extensive rights have been accorded both by legislation and by the decisions of the Court. The fact that there has been less migration between the Member States than might first have been expected, is no doubt due in part to the recession and to economic difficulties of recent years. It is, however, clear that as the Member States become more closely integrated, the recognition of these rights will be of considerable importance. The Court has undoubtedly played a major role in establishing the nature and detail of these rights.

Having moved, being treated equally

Article 48 does not, however, simply give a right of entry and a right to stay to the worker. It goes beyond that since free movement would not be very valuable if the worker who moved from one State to another could be treated differently in the host State from national

---

[22] Directive 90/365/EEC, O.J. (1990) L.180, p. 28.

workers. Accordingly, paragraph 2 of Article 48 provides that free movement entails the abolition of any discrimination based on nationality between workers of Member States as regards "employment, remuneration and other conditions of work and employment." The 1968 Regulation on the free movement of workers and the Council Directive on the abolition of restrictions on movement and residence within the Community for workers of Member States and their families have developed this principle further.[23] The influence of the Court's decisions in applying these measures and Article 48 of the Treaty has been considerable.

In the first place, the Court held that Article 48 and various provisions of the subordinate legislation are directly effective so that they can be relied upon in national courts. In the result, a worker, who feels that national legislation limits his right to equal treatment, may apply to the national court for a decision to that effect, and the Commission has used the Article 169 procedure to challenge legislation or practices which contravene this principle of equal treatment. The earliest classic case is one in which French legislation provided that a proportion of the crew of a ship had to be of French nationality. The Court accepted that both Article 48 and Regulation 1612/68 are directly effective and that the restriction was in breach of Community law. Moreover, France was not able to avoid a decision against it on the basis that administrative instructions had been given that the discriminatory provision, whilst remaining in force, should not be applied to workers from other Member States.[24]

Article 3(1) of Regulation 1612/68 itself provides that administrative practices or national provisions, even

---

[23] See note 1.
[24] Case 167/73 *Commission* v. *France* [1974] E.C.R. 359.

those applicable irrespective of nationality, are not valid if their exclusive or principal aim or effect is to exclude nationals of other Member States from employment.

The Court has emphasised that "the rules regarding equality of treatment, both in the Treaty and in Article 7 of Regulation No. 1612/68, forbid not only overt discrimination by reason of nationality but also all covert forms of discrimination which by the application of other criteria of differentiation, lead in fact to the same result."[25] And so the Court is normally quick to ensure that restrictions which appear to be applied without distinction to nationals and non-nationals do not in fact lead to different treatment for migrants from other Member States.

As part of the process of ensuring that equal treatment is observed, the Court has insisted that a form of judicial review should be available if a person concerned is refused employment. Thus, in *Heylens*,[26] a Belgian football manager wished to work in France. He was refused a licence and was then prosecuted for working as a football manager. No reasons were given for the decision and the Court held that it is essential, if equal treatment is to be secured, that there should be a form of review of the reasons given. The man or woman who is refused employment should know precisely the reasons on which refusal is based. He or she can then take the matter before a court and that court can review the legality of the decisions reached.

This need for transparency and for an independent judicial review are obviously vital in ensuring that there is equal treatment for Community nationals. Under the regulations, equal treatment is to apply not only to conditions of work but also to social and tax advantages

[25] Case 152/73 *Sotgiu* v. *Deutsche Bundespost* [1974] E.C.R. 153.
[26] Case 222/86 *UNECTEF* v. *Heylens* [1987] E.C.R. 4097.

enjoyed by national workers. "Social advantages" and "tax advantages" have been broadly interpreted so as to include all advantages whether or not attached to a contract of employment, as for example reductions in fares for large families,[27] a guaranteed minimum subsistence allowance,[28] a minimum income for old persons,[29] rights and benefits in matters of housing,[30] interest-free loans to families in respect of newborn children.[31] A migrant worker was entitled to require that criminal proceedings against him should be conducted in a language (German) other than the normal language (Flemish) of the court if national workers could insist on that.[32]

Similarly, grants in respect of university studies leading to a professional qualification constitute a "social advantage" and the national of one Member State, who pursues such university studies in another Member State after having worked in the host State, must be regarded as a worker, provided that there is a link between the previous activity and the studies in question.[33]

There are so many situations in which discrimination can occur that only a selection can be indicated. A recent case before the Court concerned a provision of Luxembourg law whereby overpaid income tax was not to be repaid if the taxpayer was not resident in Luxembourg during the entire year of assessment.[34] The Court was satisfied that although the criterion at issue was

[27] Case 32/75 *Fiorini* [1975] E.C.R. 1085.

[28] Case 249/83 *Hoeckx* [1985] E.C.R. 973.

[29] Case 261/83 *Castelli* [1984] E.C.R. 3199.

[30] Case 63/86 *Commission* v. *Italy* [1988] E.C.R. 29.

[31] Case 65/81 *Reina* [1982] E.C.R. 33.

[32] Case 137/84 *Mutsch* [1985] E.C.R. 2681.

[33] Case 39/86 *Lair* [1988] E.C.R. 3161 and Case 197/86 *Brown* [1988] E.C.R. 3205.

[34] Case C–175/88 *Biehl* [1990] E.C.R. I–1779.

permanent residence, the rule in fact worked against non-Luxembourgers. According to Advocate General Darmon, it might, in the first place, discourage someone from leaving Luxembourg to find work in another Member State and, secondly, it could discourage somebody going to Luxembourg in order to take up employment there in the middle of the year. Accordingly, the Luxembourg provision was declared to be contrary to Community law.

The Court struck down another provision of Luxembourg law in July this year.[35] The provision in question concerned elections to the governing body of a professional association responsible for defending the interests of workers and consulted on future legislation. Foreign workers were required to be affiliated and to pay contributions to the institute but had no voting rights. There was the plainest discrimination against workers from other Member States.

Occasionally a discriminatory practice is accepted for overriding reasons. The 1968 Regulation provides that the nature of the post to be filled may justify a requirement as to knowledge of a particular language. The case of *Anita Groener*[36] is particularly relevant in this context. Mrs. Groener, a Dutch national, was employed as a part-time art teacher on a temporary basis in a college in Dublin. She wanted to be appointed to a permanent full-time post. However, the Irish Constitution provides that Irish is the national language and the first official language: it is the policy of the Irish Government to protect and to promote the language on that basis. Accordingly, a certificate in the Irish language was required of someone who had not been educated in

---

[35] Case C–213/90 *Association de soutien aux travailleurs immigrés*, judgment of July 4, 1991, not yet reported.

[36] Case 379/87 *Groener* [1989] E.C.R. 3967.

the Irish language. Mrs. Groener failed the test for the certificate and so was refused the appointment.

She contended that this was a discrimination against her. It was likely to be more difficult for a non-Irish person to satisfy this provision than for an Irish national. Moreover, it was clear that the Irish language was not specifically needed for her to be able to teach art to her students. The students communicated with the teachers in English. The teachers communicated with each other in English. Books on the subject were written in English rather than in Irish. It was clear that Irish is not spoken by all the population of Ireland.

Article 3(1) of Regulation 1612/68 bans national rules or practices where "though applicable irrespective of nationality their exclusive or principal aim or effect is to keep nationals of other Member States away from the employment offered." That provision, however, is not to apply "to conditions relating to linguistic knowledge required by reason of the nature of the post to be filled." In the end, the Court accepted that, since Irish was the national language and the first official language of the country and that the measures implementing the policy were not disproportionate, given that the level demanded for the test was not very high, there was no unlawful discrimination against nationals of other Member States.

This case perhaps goes to the limits. It is a particularly strong decision since English was obviously used far more than Irish and was the second national language. Mrs. Groener was perfectly competent in English and had been able to teach on a part-time and temporary footing without any problems. The basis of the Court's decision, however, is that it is through teachers at whatever level that a language can be kept alive and developed. It was thus felt to be not unreasonable that some proficiency in Irish should be demanded. If the post had been advertised for some other profession, then different considerations would have applied. To seek to extend that decision to all civil servants or to people engaged in even the social services would, in my view, be going too far. Whether such a rule could be justified in respect of doctors is a difficult question. The answer need not be the same since, in the case of the doctor and patient, the real issue is not whether cultural reasons justify a language qualification but whether there can be adequate communication between doctor and patient and whether Irish would be required for that. For the majority of people in Ireland, it would seem that English would not only be a sufficient, but also the most efficient, method of communication. These factors all have to be balanced.

Social security and social assistance are obviously of fundamental importance to effective free movement of workers. National schemes still administer to social needs and the object of Regulation 1408/71 on social security[37] is not to harmonise national schemes but to seek to co-ordinate them in order to make sure that periods taken into account under the laws of several countries where the worker has been employed should be aggregated and to deal with the payment of benefits. These cases can be extremely complicated in assessing which country is liable to pay and in what amount and there are of course different provisions relating to different kinds of benefit. The Court has been asked on a substantial number of occasions to rule on the validity of national rules and in particular their compatibility with Regulation 1408/71. Those fully familiar with the social security legislation find a logic and a beauty in its structure. Most lawyers, however, find the legislation both of the Community and of the Member States

---

[37] O.J. (1971) L.149, p. 2. See codified version annexed to Regulation 2001/83, O.J. (1983) L.230, p. 6.

bewilderingly complex. It is difficult to see how the ordinary citizen who is not a lawyer can even begin to grapple with this legislation. It is perhaps inevitably complex. The Court has very often met with considerable difficulty in finding a way through it which is compatible with the overall objective of the Treaty—the free movement of workers. The Court is, however, conscious of the importance of this legislation as a tool for achieving that objective.

Limitations

There are some limitations on the right to free movement. Thus the Treaty itself in Article 48(3) justifies restrictions on the grounds of public policy, public security or public health. Directive 64/221[38] also lays down precise rules. The Court interprets these exemptions strictly so as to avoid Member States being able to make inroads into the overriding principle of the free movement of workers. Restrictions which are imposed must be "necessary" for the protection of national security or public safety in a democratic society. Moreover, the principle of proportionality must be respected in order to avoid discrimination on arbitrary grounds. Thus, it is only when the conduct of the individual leads to a genuine and sufficiently serious threat affecting one of the fundamental interests of society, that a Member State may invoke Article 48(3) of the Treaty.[39]

There has been in this respect a shift of emphasis on the part of the Court. Thus, in the first reference from the United Kingdom,[40] the Court accepted that it was for

[38] O.J. English Special Edition (1963–1964), p. 117.
[39] Case 30/77 *Bouchereau* [1977] E.C.R. 1999.
[40] Case 41/74 *Van Duyn* [1974] E.C.R. 1337.

the Member States to decide on social policy. At that time, the United Kingdom did not approve of the practice of scientology but it did not make that practice illegal or ban it. Accordingly, a Dutch girl who sought to enter the United Kingdom to practise scientology, and was refused admission, was unable to establish that there was a violation by the United Kingdom of any Community law right. A measure of discretion was allowed to the Member States.

More recently the Court has taken a stricter line. Thus, in a case where it was sought to deport French prostitutes from Belgium,[41] it was established that prostitution was not unlawful in Belgium, and that no steps were taken to prevent Belgian prostitutes from plying their trade. It might have been said that in this case the Member State was entitled to adopt its own social mores, as in the scientology case, and that Community rules did not impinge. The Court took a much tougher attitude and held that restrictions on free movement could not be relied on where the Member State does not "adopt, with respect to the same conduct on the part of its own nationals, repressive measures or other genuine and effective measures to combat such conduct."

It seems to me that this decision was clearly right. It also seems likely that if the scientology case had come at this time, rather than earlier, the Court might well have found that the fact that the United Kingdom did not ban or prevent the practice of scientology for its own nationals, prevented it from saying that persons should be refused entry into the United Kingdom on that ground. There must be an evenhanded suppression before one of these restrictions can be relied on to

[41] Joined Cases 115 and 116/81 *Adoui and Cornuaille* [1982] E.C.R. 1665.

prevent a Community citizen from entering a Member State in the exercise of rights which he otherwise has.

With the same objective of upholding the right of free movement, the exclusion in Article 48(4) of the Treaty, which declares that freedom of movement shall not apply to employment in the public service, has been narrowly construed. This restriction is only to apply to "posts which involve direct or indirect participation in the exercise of powers conferred by public law and duties designed to safeguard the general interest of the State or of other public authorities."[42]

FREEDOM OF MOVEMENT

The freedom of movement of workers, the right of establishment and the free provision of services, all illustrate a more general aim of the Treaty—the free movement of persons. There was, and still is, much to be done in this regard by the Commission and by the Council. Already the Council has adopted directives extending the right of residence to non-working persons, with effect from June 30, 1992,[43] and the Commission is involved in adopting other measures necessary for the achievement of the Single Market. There are undoubtedly very difficult issues to be tackled—difficult both from the political and the administrative standpoint. Thus, even whilst endorsing the overall aim of the Treaty in this respect, there are clearly strong arguments in favour of allowing Member States a measure of control to deal with terrorism, arms traffic, and drugs

---

[42] Case 149/79 *Commission* v. *Belgium* [1980] E.C.R. 3881 (interim judgment) and [1982] E.C.R. 1845. See also, Case 307/84 *Commission* v. *France* [1986] E.C.R. 1725 and Case 225/85 *Commission* v. *Italy* [1987] E.C.R. 2625.

[43] Directives 90/364, 90/365 and 90/366, O.J. (1990) L.180, pp. 26, 28 and 30.

traffic at the external borders of the Community. It is plain that great care has to be exercised in balancing the right of citizens of the Member States to move around with the compelling need to avoid giving freedom of entry to terrorists and to those smuggling drugs and arms.

All these many aspects of the free movement of workers go far to illustrate how important the rules of Community law are to the private citizen. If he had thought in 1973 that the Treaty would not impinge on the lives of people, the Danish national, recently before the Court would have been very surprised to find himself there.[44] He worked in Germany but went back almost daily to Denmark, where his girlfriend lived, and he visited her in a car registered in Germany. Because he visited Denmark so frequently, the Danish authorities considered that he had transferred his normal residence to Denmark. They confiscated his car on the grounds that it had not been registered in Denmark. The Court of Justice held that the mere fact that he went back to Denmark from the place where he had found a job and a dwelling, even if every night and every weekend, was not enough to support the conclusion that he had transferred his normal residence to Denmark.

It is in this sort of case that the Court finds itself very much in touch with daily life.

Perhaps one of the most interesting cases involving the individual which has occurred in the last few years was the case of *Cowan*.[45] In that case, an Englishman, who was visiting Paris, was assaulted at the exit of a Metro station. He applied for a form of criminal injury compensation and was refused on the grounds that he was neither a French national nor a foreign national

---

[44] Case C–297/89 *Ryborg*, judgment of April 23, 1991, not yet reported.
[45] Case 186/87 *Cowan* [1989] E.C.R. 195.

whose State had concluded a reciprocal agreement with France for the application of criminal injury compensation rules. Accordingly, Mr. Cowan claimed that this rule was discriminatory, contrary to Article 7 of the Treaty, which provides that:

> "Within the scope of application of this Treaty, and without prejudice to any special provisions contained therein, any discrimination on grounds of nationality shall be prohibited."

The real question was whether there was here discrimination within the scope or application of the Treaty. The Court recalled that the freedom to provide services included the freedom for the recipients of services to go to another Member State in order to receive them there, without obstruction. Tourists, among others, must be regarded as recipients of services.[46] It followed that, when Community law guaranteed a natural person the freedom to go to another Member State, compensation for harm in that State, paid on the same basis as to nationals and persons residing there, is "a corollary of that freedom of movement." Accordingly, the French provision was held to be discriminatory. Even though the legislative provisions concerned criminal acts, such provisions "may not discriminate against persons to whom Community law gives a right to equal treatment or restrict the fundamental freedoms guaranteed by Community law."

On this aspect, I have deliberately concentrated on the jurisprudence of the Court. There are, however, issues which are highly relevant to individuals in which the Court alone cannot, and perhaps should not have to, deal. These issues are to be resolved either by

[46] Joined Cases 266/82 and 26/83, *supra.*

Community regulations and directives or by inter-governmental agreements between the Member States; preferably, if further integration is to be achieved, by the former, which are, of course, subject to judicial review by the Court of Justice.

Some of these issues have recently been dealt with. The Council, pursuant to Article 235 of the Treaty, has recently adopted three directives on the right of residence in respect of students, pensioners and those who are not economically active. The scope of these directives thus extends far beyond the category of workers and those who provide services or seek to establish themselves. These are important steps but the Community is still far from giving a right of residence across the board to all nationals of the Member States and it is not, at this stage, clear how far the principle of equality of treatment applies to the groups upon whom rights of residence are now conferred. There is plainly both need and scope here for further judicial interpreta-tion.

But there are other and different issues. Controls at the external borders of the Member States, policies on visas and on asylum, need to be resolved if drug dealers and terrorists are not to gain unintended advantages from the creation of an internal market. Harmonisation, or at any rate co-ordination, of extradition policy, of policing and of the criminal law, at any rate in some areas, will become increasingly necessary. In my view, these matters need to be dealt with by legislation in a way which provides the European Court of Justice with a jurisdiction to interpret and review the validity of what is done.

The Schengen Agreement, now adopted by all the founding Member States of the Community, provides for some such matters—co-operation on law enforcement, harmonisation of rules on the crossing of external frontiers, the issuing of visas. The Dublin Convention, signed by all the Member States except Denmark, deals with the question of asylum. But they are both only first steps to tackling major problems relating to the movement both of citizens and non-citizens of the Member States in a Community without internal frontiers.

From all of this it is clear that, in facilitating the free movement of employed persons, the Community has provided the opportunity for the worker's integration into the new social and economic environment by granting to him (and his family) a right of residence, social security benefits and other social advantages.

THE PROFESSIONS

"Workers" are not the only economically-active groups concerned by free movement. Establishment and the provision of services in another Member State are of considerable importance, particularly to the development of the internal market. Articles 52 and 59 provide for the abolition of restrictions on establishment and the provision of services within the framework of the provisions set out in Chapter 2 of Title III of the Treaty. The Court has built up a body of law dealing with these matters. I look, by way of example, only at one aspect, namely the situation of the liberal professions.

Although, as a result of the operation of Article 59, prospective clients travel more freely from one Member State to another in order to consult the professional adviser of their choice, difficulties arise when the professional person wishes to move—either temporarily or permanently—to another Member State. The barriers to free movement arise from the regulation of the professions by the Member States either by requiring a particular diploma or by limiting the exercise of the profession to those qualifying for a particular title.

The Community is, of course, aware of the difficulties standing in the way of, for example, a doctor, a lawyer or a physiotherapist who wants to move from one Member State to another and has taken legislative steps to remove them. The initial approach was to proceed by a series of directives, each dealing individually with a single profession harmonising the education and training throughout the Community and providing for automatic recognition of the different national diplomas. By 1987, when this approach was abandoned, only seven such directives—mostly covering medical professions—had been adopted. The new approach which is, for the moment, embodied in Directive 48/89 (and which is largely due to the initiative of Lord Cockfield, the British Commissioner) consists in creating general systems for the recognition of *all* diplomas and professional qualifications of a certain level. The first "layer" of qualifications to be so dealt with are those acquired after three or more years of higher education. Directive 48/89 came into force on January 4, 1991, but, at the date of this lecture, only two Member States—the United Kingdom and Ireland —had adopted the necessary implementing legislation.

Obviously, seen from the point of view of the individual, the situation, prior to the coming into force of Directive 48/89, was far from satisfactory unless he or she happened to be a member of one of the few professions which were covered by a sectoral directive. Community secondary legislation offered no assistance in the result.

Over the last 15 years or so, the Court has been asked to rule on the application of Article 52 of the Treaty to cases not covered by subordinate legislation. Its case law is now of considerable assistance to a Community national who, holding a professional qualification from one Member State, wishes to live and work in another.

The first of two of these cases were decided by the Court in 1977.

The first case concerned a Belgian lawyer, Maître Thieffry, who had obtained a doctorate in Belgian law and had been admitted to the Brussels bar.[47] He took steps to obtain recognition in France of his Belgian qualifications. His Belgian doctorate was recognised by the Sorbonne as equivalent to the French "licence en droit." He obtained the French professional qualification, the CAPA. He then sought admission to the Paris bar. His application was rejected on the grounds that French law required members of the bar to hold a French university degree. The French Court of Appeal asked the Court to decide whether a national rule of this kind was to be considered contrary to the Treaty in the absence of any Community measure providing for the mutual recognition of legal qualifications.

The Court emphasised that the directives providing for mutual recognition of diplomas, envisaged by Article 57, were intended to assist individuals seeking to exercise the fundamental right of freedom of establishment, guaranteed to them by Article 52. In the absence of such measures, the Member States were bound by Article 5 of the Treaty to secure freedom of establishment. "It is," the Court said, "incumbent upon the competent public authorities—including legally recognised professional bodies—to ensure that such practice or legislation is applied in accordance with the objective ... of the Treaty relating to freedom of establishment." A rule refusing admission to a profession to a person holding a diploma recognised as equivalent to the national diploma solely on the grounds of the diploma's foreign origin was contrary to Community law. The distinction made in national law between the academic effect and the civil

[47] Case 71/76 *Thieffry* [1977] E.C.R. 765.

effect of the recognition of a foreign diploma did not, *per se*, justify the refusal to recognise such equivalence as evidence of professional qualification. Although the precise effects of the recognition accorded to Thieffry's Belgian degree by the Sorbonne was a matter for the national authorities, the Court made it clear that "the recognition of evidence of a professional qualification for the purposes of establishment may be accepted to the full extent compatible with the observance of professional requirements."

Similarly, in *Patrick*,[48] the Court was able to "graft" Community law rights onto existing national provisions under French law; foreign-qualified architects were entitled to practise in France, on production of a diploma equivalent to that required for French architects and subject to reciprocal rights being granted to French nationals in the country awarding the diploma. Although the British architects' qualification had been recognised as equivalent by ministerial decree, Patrick, a British architect, was refused admission to the French profession on the ground that there was no convention of reciprocity between France and the United Kingdom. The Court rejected an attempt by France to argue that, in the absence of a Community directive providing for the mutual recognition of diplomas, the Treaty could not be a substitute for the convention required under French law. The absence of an appropriate directive did not entitle the Member State to deny the practical benefit of freedom of establishment when that freedom could be secured by virtue of the provisions of the laws and regulations already in force in the Member State in question.

Whereas in *Thieffrey* and *Patrick*, there already existed *de facto* recognition of the equivalence between the

---

[48] Case 11/77 [1977] E.C.R. 1199.

national and the foreign qualification, in the more recent case of *Vlassopoulou*, the applicant was faced with a national system which made no provision for the recognition of foreign qualifications.

Under German law, the only route open to a foreign-qualified lawyer wishing to establish himself in Germany was to requalify in accordance with national regulations.[49] Miss Vlassopoulou, a Greek lawyer who possessed a doctorate[50] in law from Tübingen University, had lived and worked in Germany for a number of years. She was, as a "Rechtsbeistand,"[51] entitled to advise on Greek and European law. She applied for, and was refused, admission to the German bar. The German Government argued that, in the absence of Community rules, it was entitled to apply the national, non-discriminatory rules on admission to the bar. The question was thus asked, for the first time, whether Article 52 would assist an individual in such circumstances.

The Court, having referred to the duty of the Member States under Article 5 of the Treaty to take "all appropriate measures ... to ensure fulfilment of the obligations arising out of the Treaty," pointed out that national regulations concerning qualifications, even where applied indistinctly, might nevertheless obstruct nationals of other Member States wishing to exercise their right of freedom of establishment. Such would be the case where the national rules failed to take account of knowledge and qualifications already acquired by the individual elsewhere in the Community. It followed that

---

[49] The German Government in the observations submitted to the Court pointed out that the position would change when the regulation implementing Directive 48/89 came into force.

[50] Doctorates in Germany, as in the United Kingdom, are of purely academic value and do not entitle the holder to practise law.

[51] Literally "legal assistant."

where a Member State was faced with a request to practise a regulated profession, it was required to compare the skills and knowledge attested to by the diplomas produced by the applicant with those required by national law. Where the diploma showed that its holder possessed equivalent qualifications, the applicant was to be allowed to practise in the host Member State. If there was a partial equivalence there should be a partial recognition.

The judgment permits national authorities to take into account differences in the professional "environment" between Member States. Thus, for example, in relation to the legal profession, a Member State is entitled to decide that the study of, say, land law in one legal system cannot be considered as equivalent to the study of the same subject elsewhere. Our own is very different from that of most Member States and "equivalence" is out of the question. Likewise, where the national rules demand a period of supervised practical training or of practice (such as pupillage or articles) and the applicant has not actually undergone that training, the host Member State is required to consider whether a period of professional experience, either in the Member State of origin or in the host Member State, is reasonably equivalent. It is no use just saying, "I did ten years in a lawyer's office and articles take two years, therefore I need not do articles." What sort of work the person did during the 10 years is relevant to see whether the experience and training matches what would be gained from articles. Ten years in divorce work is not the equivalent of two years covering litigation, company flotations, personal injuries and commercial contracts. The national authorities are entitled to require the applicant to show that he has acquired the necessary skills and qualifications. In practice, this is likely to mean that the applicant will be asked to pass the professional

examination in those subjects where his existing knowledge is deficient.

It is for the national courts to decide whether the
judgment assists Miss Vlassopoulou to obtain admission.
Despite some similarities between Greek and German
law (especially in relation to Greek criminal law and the
law of civil procedure), her academic studies and
practical experience, she may still be faced with a
number of examinations in German law.

However, taking a broader view, it is clear that the
legal profession is more nationally orientated than most
others—a lawyer's training reflects the fact that there are
12 (or 13, if one counts Scotland) separate legal systems
within the Community. Where the applicant is an
engineer, a physiotherapist, a teacher or an accountant,
the Court's judgment in *Vlassopoulou* is likely to be
relevant. Although the judgment may be somewhat
overtaken by the application of Directive 48/89, it
remains important in two respects. In the first place, it
will be relevant for those professions not covered by that
directive or by a sectoral directive. In the second place,
the judgment represents a baseline against which the
measures implementing Directive 48/89 will fall to be
judged. The Directive, like the judgment, allows Member
States to demand ''topping up'' where the migrant
professional person's training does not cover all the
national requirements. Since, however, the Directive's
raison d'être is to improve upon the situation created by
the direct effect of Articles 5 and 52, any ''topping up''
requirements imposed in reliance upon it will have to be
less than those which Member States would be entitled
to require as a result of the *Vlassopoulou* judgment.

Parallel to these cases are others where restrictive rules
have been struck down. Thus, the French rule requiring
a doctor, who wanted to practise in Paris, or to act as a
locum, or even to visit patients there, to be struck off the

medical register in his own State was condemned.[52] Similarly, an attempt by the Conseil de l'Ordre des Avocats de Paris to refuse admission to the bar to a German lawyer with the necessary French degree and bar examinations, simply because he had an office in Germany (two principal offices not being allowed in France because of the obligation to have a principal office in the jurisdiction of the relevant court) was firmly rejected.[53]

Even if only a fraction of the population is going to rely on these rules as to free movement for the purposes of work, there is no doubt that the Court's rulings on equal treatment have affected substantially a large number of people.

Equality between men and women

Although Article 119 falls within Title III of the Treaty, "social policy," it is well known that the representatives of the future Member States considered the inclusion of an equal treatment rule to be necessary on economic grounds: its existence was intended to prevent a State, which extended guarantees of equal pay to female workers, from suffering a competitive disadvantage. Nevertheless, 35 years on, when the continuing inequalities between men and women provide a frequent topic of debate, the unequivocal guarantee of equal pay for men and women to be found in Article 119 appears remarkably farsighted. As a legislative provision, the years have shown Article 119 to be insufficient—it is confined to pay and fails to address discrimination in the other terms and conditions of employment. It is limited to discrimination within the employment relationship

---

[52] Case 96/85 *Commission* v. *France* [1986] E.C.R. 1475.
[53] Case 107/83 *Klopp* [1984] E.C.R. 2971.

and therefore fails to take account of discriminatory measures emanating from the State as, for example, in the areas of tax or social security legislation. Finally, it does not extend to positive measures intended to improve women's employment prospects and job security, such as minimum child care provisions or parental leave.

On the other hand, as a weapon in the judicial armoury, Article 119 has proved most effective and the Court's case law has contributed significantly to the development of equal opportunity law. The Court's approach has been marked, first, by its extensive interpretation of the concept of "pay." This has the effect of reducing the need for secondary legislation—which the Council often finds it difficult to agree upon—and increases the scope for actions relying directly upon Article 119, which is important in the light of the limits on the direct effect of directives.

Article 119 provides that pay includes, in addition to the ordinary basic or minimum wage or salary, "any other consideration, whether in cash or in kind, which the worker receives, directly or indirectly, in respect of his employment from his employer." This has been interpreted to include benefits received after the employee has retired, such as special travel facilities,[54] a severance grant paid on retirement,[55] and redundancy payments whether paid voluntarily, under a contract or as required by statute.[56] Most important, the concept of pay has been held to extend, not only to pensions payable from an occupational scheme financed by the

---

[54] Case 12/84 *Garland* v. *British Railways Board* [1982] E.C.R. 555.
[55] Case C–33/89 *Kowalska* v. *Freie und Hansestadt Hamburg* [1990] E.C.R. I–2591.
[56] Case C–262/88 *Barber* v. *Guardian Royal Exchange Assurance Group* [1990] E.C.R. I–1889.

employer,[57] but also to occupational schemes financed jointly by employer and employee contributions. That is so, even where the scheme substitutes in part for the retirement pension provided by the national social security system. The Court, in *Barber*, also found that the prohibition on discrimination in relation to pension schemes implied not merely that the rate of pension paid should be the same for men and women but also that the terms of access to the pension should be the same. Thus differential qualifying ages—even where they respect the statutory pension system—are unacceptable. The Court's ruling may be contrasted with the terms of Directive 86/378 on the implementation of the principle of equal treatment for men and women in occupational social security schemes,[58] which authorised Member States to defer the compulsory implementation of the principle of equalisation of pensionable age in such schemes. The Court was aware that, at the time of its judgment, a proposed directive which would have removed this derogation from the principle of equal treatment, had been pending before the Council of Ministers for three years with no prospect of immediate agreement. Had such an agreement been reached, changes would have been planned or effected in private pension schemes much earlier.

The Court has not only given an extensive interpretation of "pay," it has also declared that Article 119 has direct effect.[59] Individuals are thus able to rely directly on Article 119 in actions brought before national courts, even where the relevant national legislation purports to restrict their rights to equal pay. Since the principle of

[57] Case 170/84 *Bilka-Kaufhaus* [1986] E.C.R. 1607.

[58] O.J. (1986) L.225, p. 40, Corrigendum published in O.J. (1986) L.283, p. 27.

[59] Case 43/75 *Defrenne* v. *Sabena* [1976] E.C.R. 455.

equal pay is contained in an article of the Treaty, its direct effects are both "vertical" and "horizontal"; in other words, Article 119 may be pleaded in aid in actions brought against both the State and private individuals. As already explained, the same may be true of the provisions of regulations which are sufficiently precise. Conversely, equal opportunity rights contained in directives—such as the right to equal treatment at work, the right to equal pay for work of equal value and equal rights in social security matters—cannot give rise to horizontal direct effects and cannot therefore be relied upon in a case brought against a private employer.

The equal treatment and equal value directives are possibly the parts of Community legislation which have the greatest impact on individuals in their dealings with each other. It was, perhaps, no coincidence that it was in an equal opportunity case that the Court had to make clear its position as to whether directives could have horizontal direct effect. Despite the temptation to reinforce the legal protection of the individual—a recurrent theme in the case law—the Court decided the issue in *Marshall*[60] against horizontal direct effect.

Although undoubtedly right on the language of Article 189 and in principle—why should an innocent employer be required to remedy the default of a Member State and meet the requirements of a directive which has either not been implemented at all or has been incorrectly implemented[61]—the decision means that the employee in private industry is at a disadvantage compared with the official. The decision's adverse impact on individual employment rights has, however, been tempered in two ways. First, the Court insists that national law be

---

[60] Case 152/84 [1986] E.C.R. 723.
[61] And the latter case may require detailed comparison with and interpretation of the relevant national and Community provisions.

interpreted to give effect to Community law. In *Von Colson*,[62] a case concerning the equal treatment directive, the Court stated that national courts are required to interpret the provisions of a national law, specifically introduced to give effect to a directive, in the light of the wording and the purpose of the directive. More recently, in *Marleasing*,[63] the Court held that national judges, when applying national law, should always take account of the text and objectives of the directive and should interpret national provisions accordingly, even where these pre-date the Community measure. As I made clear in my Opinion in the *Marshall* case, I have reservations about this as a general proposition. I find it difficult to say that a statute of 1870 must be interpreted in the light of a 1991 directive. If the former is in conflict with the latter, it is not for judges to strain language but for Governments to introduce new legislation. They must repeal or amend the earlier legislation. If they do not do so they may be in breach of the Treaty and the Commission should take proceedings under Article 169 of the Treaty.

Secondly, the Court in *Foster*[64] took a broad view of what constitutes a State body: it includes any organisation or authority

"which has been made responsible, pursuant to a measure adopted by the State, for providing a public service under the control of the State and has for that purpose special powers beyond those which result from the normal rules applicable in relations between individuals."

[62] Case 14/83 [1984] E.C.R. 1891.
[63] Case C–106/89 *Marleasing* v. *La Comercial Internacional de Alimentacíon* [1990] E.C.R. I–4135.
[64] Case C–188/89 *Foster* v. *British Gas* [1990] E.C.R. I–3313.

Employees of such bodies will be able, in appropriate circumstances, to rely either on Article 119 or on the various directives in actions brought against their employer.

The Court has recognised that it is necessary to balance individual employment rights against the far-reaching economic effects of its judgments. It limited the effects in time of its rulings in *Defrenne* and *Barber* even though, on an Article 177 reference, the Treaty gives it no express power to do so. In *Barber*, for example, the existence and terms of Directive 86/378 was recognised to have given rise to a reasonable belief that Article 119 did not apply to pensions paid under contracted-out schemes and that derogations from the principle of equality between men and women were still permitted in that sphere. The Court concluded, therefore, that

> "overriding considerations of legal certainty preclude legal situations which have exhausted all their effects in the past from being called in question where that might upset retroactively the financial balance of many contracted-out pension schemes."

In both *Defrenne* and *Barber*, those who had already lodged their claim were not subject to the limitation in time of the effects of the judgments.[65] This part of the judgment has given much trouble and indeed anxiety to small businesses, as well as to large enterprises, not only in the United Kingdom but elsewhere. It is said to be not

---

[65] The French version of the relevant part of the judgment is of no assistance here: "des considérations impérieuses de sécurité juridique s'opposent à ce que des situations juridiques qui ont épuisé leurs effets dans le passé soient remises en cause, alors que, dans un tel cas l'équilibre financier de nombre de régimes de pensions conventionellement exclus risquerait d'être retroactivement boule-versé."

clear, for example, whether the benefits of the *Barber* judgment apply only to those acquiring entitlement to pension after May 17, 1990 (the date of the judgment), or apply to those already in receipt of a pension in respect of benefits paid after that date or, as some would like to see, only to those entering into pensionable employment after that date. The question also arises as to whether the use of actuarial tables, which make allowances for the different life expectancies of men and women to calculate benefits, is compatible with the Treaty.[66] These questions will have to be resolved.

In the case of *Danfoss*,[67] the Court made use of an evidentiary rule in support of the principle of equal opportunity. Here, the female staff of a company were seeking to rely on Directive 75/117 and the principle of equal pay for work of equal value. They were able to show that the average pay of female employees of Danfoss was 6.85 per cent. lower than the average pay of male employees. However, they were frustrated in their attempts to prove individual instances of discrimination by the complicated salary structure of the firm, which provided for a basic salary and a number of bonuses. The criteria on which bonuses were awarded were not known to the staff nor was it possible to determine how much of the final salary consisted of bonuses. It was, accordingly, impossible to show that a difference in pay between any female employee and a specific male colleague was caused by discrimination. The Court found that, in situations such as this, which could be characterised by a complete lack of transparency, once the female employee had established a

---

[66] These issues are amongst those raised in Case C–200/91 *Coloroll Pension Trustees Ltd.* v. *Russell and Others*, a reference from the Chancery Division of the High Court.

[67] Case 109/88 [1989] E.C.R. 3199.

difference between the average salaries of men and women, the burden of proof shifted and the onus was on the employer to demonstrate that his salary structure was not in fact discriminatory. Any other solution would, in the view of the Court, deprive women of any effective means of ensuring that the principle of equal pay was enforced.[68]

The theme that transparency is essential for effective judicial control was also taken up in the *Barber* judgment. One of the questions before the Court was whether the equality of pay could be assessed on an overall basis taking into account all benefits in cash and kind (provision of a car, length of holidays, grants for training) or whether each individual element of the remuneration package had to be equal. The Court opted for the second alternative: it felt that an overall assessment and comparison (which might involve weighing, say, three or four days extra leave entitlement against a few pounds a month extra salary) would make judicial review difficult and the effectiveness of Article 119 would be reduced as a result.

On a different note, Article 119 provides an excellent example of the way in which Community law can have an impact on English law. It also illustrates the role played by Article 177 references. About one-third of the references in equal opportunity cases come from the United Kingdom whereas, overall, the United Kingdom produces rather fewer references than one might expect.[69] The amount of litigation in this area is

[68] This judgment anticipates, to some degree, the proposed directive on the reversal of the burden of proof in equal opportunities cases (O.J. C.176 of July 5, 1988, p. 5). The British, Portuguese and Italian Governments, which submitted observations in *Danfoss*, all supported the approach eventually taken by the Court.

[69] For example, in 1990, 12 out of 141 preliminary rulings (around 8.5 per cent.) came from the United Kingdom.

explained in part, perhaps, by the high proportion of working women in the British population but also by the existence of the Equal Opportunities Commission which has been able to identify, and provide the necessary financial backing for, suitable test cases. The Commission, to which there is no completely parallel organisation in other countries (Ireland is the nearest), has, in my view, done important work in bringing these cases before the national courts and thus eventually before the European Court. The fact that it sometimes loses is not a criticism of its work. Its job is to push back the frontiers of discrimination and if it sometimes goes too far, then it has to be told so. Its contentions may in some cases merely be premature! On the other hand, the fact that there are, relatively, so many references of this kind does not mean that the United Kingdom has the worst record. It may not, in this area, have the best. I am quite sure that in practice, it is no worse than that of many of the others.

There are many other aspects of Community law which impinge on the lives of individuals and which one could consider in detail, not least the developments, both in the Treaty, the legislation and in the Court's judgments, relating to the protection of the environment. I conclude, however, with another area which is of present interest and future importance—education.

Do students as such have any rights under Community law?

A distinction has to be drawn between workers and their families who wish to study in the host country and persons who are not already workers but who nonetheless wish to study in a Community country of which they are not nationals.

Since workers and their families already enjoy rights under the Treaty and under secondary legislation, in particular Regulation 1612/68,[70] it has been a comparatively simple matter to assimilate them to nationals of the host country as regards access to education. That is part of the process of integrating them into the host country. Regulation 1612/68 grants the migrant worker not just the right to the same social advantages as the national worker but, specifically, the same rights of access to training in vocational schools and retraining centres.[71] The children of migrant workers residing in the territory of the Member State are to be given the same rights of access to the State's general educational, apprenticeship and vocational training courses under the same conditions as the nationals of that State.[72]

The Court has interpreted these provisions to mean that a migrant worker who wishes to pursue a course of university studies leading to a professional qualification is entitled to a maintenance grant on the same condition as nationals of the host Member State.[73] This applies even if the migrant worker wishes to pursue a course in a third country,[74] provided of course that nationals of the host State would be entitled to the grant in analogous circumstances.

There is obviously a theoretical problem here. If a migrant worker undertakes a course of full-time education for which he wishes to receive a grant, does he not cease to be a worker, thereby disentitling himself to rely on the Community provisions in favour of migrant workers? Up till now the Court has sought to resolve

[70] See note 1.
[71] Article 7.
[72] Article 12.
[73] See, in particular the judgments in Case 39/86 *Lair* v. *University of Hannover* [1988] E.C.R. 3161 and Case 197/86 *Brown* v. *Secretary of State for Scotland* [1988] E.C.R. 3205.
[74] Case 235/87 *Matteucci* v. *Communauté française de Belgique* [1988] E.C.R. 5585.

this dilemma by holding that the applicant for a grant can still rely on his status as a migrant worker provided either that there is some link or continuity between his previous work and the course of study which he wishes to undertake or that he is seeking retraining in another field of activity following his becoming involuntarily unemployed.[75]

This compromise is in its turn subject to objections. Why should not a person who wishes to retrain in another trade or activity, maybe to avoid unemployment, maybe to do a better but different job, have the same assistance as persons training in their existing field of activity or those already unemployed?[76]

The children of migrant workers, who are also entitled to equal rights of access to education, have also been assimilated. As with workers themselves, the children of migrant workers can claim a grant for study in their own home country, if nationals of the host State would be entitled in similar circumstances.[77]

However, whilst workers and their families have been able to claim equal rights to education as part of the general bundle of rights which they enjoy under the freedom of movement provisions of the Treaty, the same is not true for persons who are not workers but who nonetheless wish to study in another Member State. At first sight, Community law does not seem to promise very much to them. Education is not mentioned in the Treaty as falling within the competence of the Community. Indeed it is generally recognised as remaining within the province of the Member States. However,

[75] *Lair, supra.*

[76] See, *inter alia,* the Opinion of Advocate General Van Gerven in Case C–357/89 *Raulin* v. *Dutch Minister of Education and Science,* case pending.

[77] Case 308/89 *Carmina di Leo* v. *Land Berlin* [1990] E.C.R. 4185.

Article 128 empowers the Council to lay down general principles for implementing a common vocational training policy and as early as 1963, the Council adopted a decision laying down such general principles.[78]

It is those provisions, in conjunction with the general prohibition on discrimination contained in Article 7 of the Treaty, which have led to developments at least in the field of further and higher education. In the case of *Gravier* v. *City of Liège*[79] in 1985, the Court held that the imposition by Belgium of charges or registration fees payable by nationals of other Member States as a condition of access to vocational training (in this particular case a course in strip cartoon art) was prohibited by the Treaty as being discriminatory when such a charge was not imposed on Belgian nationals. Despite all the arguments to the contrary about the true, and somewhat esoteric, nature of university education, the Court has since accepted that university studies presumptively constitute vocational training. There may be exceptions in the case of certain courses of study intended simply to improve a student's general knowledge.[80] Effectively, however, Member States may not discriminate between their own nationals and nationals of other Member States as regards the conditions of access, whether financial or otherwise, to university education.

The line between prohibiting discrimination on the basis of Community law and not trespassing on areas of education and social policy, which are the prerogative of the Member States, is not always easy to draw. Thus, in

---

[78] Council Decision of April 2, 1963, laying down general principles for implementing a common vocational training policy, Official Journal, English Special Edition (1963–1964), p. 25.

[79] Case 293/83 [1985] E.C.R. 593.

[80] Case 24/86 *Blaizot* v. *University of Liège* [1988] E.C.R. 379.

1988, the Court held that grants to students fell outside the Treaty except to the extent to which such financial assistance was actually intended to defray registration or tuition fees charged for access to such education.[81] It is only these fees which are treated as creating a barrier to access to vocational training. This again represents something of a compromise. On one view, it is difficult to distinguish between a maintenance grant and reimbursement of specific fees charged, since a student who does not receive the maintenance grant may be just as impeded from pursuing a course of study as one who does not have his registration fees waived or reimbursed. Such a rule may also give rise to practical problems of application if a Member State simply makes a lump sum grant without stating what proportion, if any, of that grant is intended to reimburse education fees and what proportion is intended to cover a student's basic living expenses. This problem has arisen in a case currently before the Court.[82] Yet the objection that substantial maintenance grants (especially if payable by local authorities) should not fall to be paid to non-nationals has much force and pragmatically it is justified to treat such grants as falling outside the prohibition on discrimination.

The Court has thus had to be cautious in these cases involving the recognition of rights to students who are not also workers. An area which is even more sensitive than that of student grants is the question whether foreign students who have been admitted to follow a course of study in a Member State automatically obtain the right of residence in that State for the duration of the course or whether they are dependent on national law for any right of residence. Conscious of this problem and

[81] *Brown, supra.*
[82] *Raulin, supra.*

taking account of the judgments of the Court prohibiting discrimination in regard to access to vocational training, the Council adopted a directive on the rights of residence for students which must be transposed not later than June 30, 1992.[83] Under the directive, Member States are required to grant the right of residence to students but the right is restricted to the duration of the course of studies in question and may be accompanied by various other conditions. In adopting the directive, however, the Council regarded itself as obliged to rely on Article 235 since, in its view, the Treaty, in particular Articles 7 and 128, did not provide the necessary powers for the directive to be adopted. Because of this the directive has now been challenged by the Parliament, which considers that the directive could have been adopted without invoking Article 235, which requires that the Parliament be consulted rather than the full co-operation procedure set out in Article 149 of the Treaty.[84]

It may be an open question whether the directive was necessary in order to grant the right of residence to students or whether the right of residence flows directly from the Treaty in the light of the Court's earlier case law on student rights. In fact this question is currently before the Court[85] and it has been argued, in particular by the Commission, that the right of residence of a student in the host Member State is a natural corollary of his right to be admitted to vocational training in that State on the same condition as nationals. Needless to say, this view has not commended itself to all of the Member States,[86] some of which still regard rights of

---

[83] Council Directive 90/366/EEC of June 28, 1990, on the right of residence for students, O.J. (1990) L.180, p. 30.

[84] Case C–295/90 *Parliament* v. *Council*, case pending.

[85] *Raulin, supra.*

[86] In particular the United Kingdom.

residence as being too sensitive a matter to be established simply by implication from other rights.

At the same time, the Commission and the Council have also been taking an interest in the universities as part of the implementation of a common vocational training policy. Apart from the provision of the Jean Monnet professorships financed by the Community, the ERASMUS programme and the COMET programme are being implemented. The ERASMUS programme seeks to promote co-operation between universities in all Member States and to encourage students to spend a part of their course in a Member State other than their own. The programme has what might be termed economic, intellectual and social goals and the Court upheld the validity of the programme (in which reliance needed to be placed on Article 235) in 1989.[87] The COMET II programme is not a purely inter-university programme but a programme on co-operation between universities and industry regarding training in the field of technology, which was also challenged and recently upheld by the Court on the basis that the necessary powers flowed directly from the Treaty, in particular those relating to vocational training.[88]

Free movement, equality of treatment, both as between nationals and as between the sexes, in employment, in social security, in education, are all facets of this newly-created system of law which affects our daily lives.[89] The preamble to the Treaty, the "task" and "activities" of the Community, made it clear that social as well as purely economic changes would be made. This

[87] Case 242/87 *Commission* v. *Council* [1989] E.C.R. 1425.
[88] Joined Cases C–51, C–90 and C–94/89 *United Kingdom, France and Germany* v. *Council*, judgment of June 11, 1991, not yet reported.
[89] See generally, Anthony Arnull, "The General Principles of EEC Law and the Individual" (1990, Leicester University Press).

introduction to the developments which have already taken place show how far we have gone. It was, perhaps, inevitable in this area as much as in any other that controversy would arise. The Social Charter, not legally binding, is hotly contested and there are clearly those who wish at all costs to prevent what they regard as Community interference in the "nooks and crannies" of social affairs. The Court will, I have no doubt, continue to give effect to the Treaty. The rest is for the politicians and the voters.

4. ADAPTING TO CHANGE

Albeit, as I have shown, the achievements of the Court have been substantial, even seminal, in the development of the Community, yet there is no cause to sit back. Just as in a developing Community the law will not stand still—there must be adjustment and change—so the Court cannot stand still. Its rules, its working methods, were first developed when there were six Member States, when cases were few and when the Court held hearings on only a few days a month. The position is now very different. Not far short of 400 new cases have been arriving at the Court each year, though in 1990/91 the number was down to 335. Allowing for 200 judgments and, on average, 130 withdrawals or summary dismissals, the backlog can only increase, and by September 1991 the "stock" of cases before the Court and the Court of First Instance amounted to 782, of which 614 were before the Court. The Court decided that Chambers would sit regularly on Fridays, leaving Tuesday to Thursday for the full Court. Friday is no longer reserved for the délibérés of the full Court. That has been found to cause too much delay in the hearing of Chambers cases so that as from February, Chambers cases will be taken on Thursdays, and Fridays will be reserved for the délibérés of the full Court. It may not be long before Monday is under threat.

This caseload limits the time which can be spent by members of the Court and their associates on each case. It imposes too heavy a burden on them if they are to think out in depth the issues for decision (and there is little point in the House of Lords or the Cour de Cassation sending a question to Luxembourg unless it can be considered in depth); it results in unacceptable delays.

The current delays cause concern—16 months rather than six months 15 years ago for an answer to a national court's questions and over 20 months for a direct action—although it has to be borne in mind that in many of the Member States this time scale is not particularly shocking since the time taken from the beginning to the end of cases before national courts can be much longer. It is, however, on any view unsatisfactory that national courts should have to wait so long for a reply before they can proceed to a decision in the cases pending before them.

If the burden on the judges increases further that should cause no less concern. Even if the role of a trial judge above all is to be "quick, courteous and right," since if he is wrong he can be corrected on appeal, "hurry, hurry, hurry" should not be the motto of a court which, in respect of the law it administers, is final and supreme and which, in respect of some classes of case, is the only forum available to litigants.

It is easy for courts, like other administrations, to become complacent and to accept defects and delays as being part of the nature of things. This Court is certainly not complacent about the need for change, and change there must be. The Court will not stand still. The difficulty is to find time to really think out what change is needed. Recently, much thought has been given to the subject—to get 19 fairly individualistic people to agree about anything, let alone change, is very time-consuming and may in itself contain the seeds of a necessary change.

I do not say that my views—initially conditioned by my immersion in the English legal system—are representative of the Court, of a majority, or indeed of a recognisable minority of its members, and indeed the kaleidoscopic pattern changes as different issues arise for discussion. On some questions we may be unanimous, or I may be one of the majority, in a minority, or wholly eccentric. Nothing I say gives any clue as to what my colleagues or any of them think. Indeed, I prefer to suggest areas for consideration rather than solutions and these only by way of example.

The starting point is the scope of the Court's jurisdiction. As the workload grew over the years, the Court realised that it would not be able to do everything. Staff cases—claims by officials against the European institutions, their employers—provided an obvious category to be removed. The cases were very important to the individuals and sometimes gave rise to pronouncements on important issues of law which could have wider relevance than to staff cases. Many of them, however, were not very difficult: these would have been better resolved by a tribunal with experience of industrial law questions or, at any rate, having more time to hear witnesses, to investigate facts. So, many years ago, a proposal was made for a tribunal to deal with these cases. Some people did not like the idea—they thought that officials had the right to go direct, rather than on appeal, to the Community's own administrative law court. Other people preferred to have a tribunal with representatives of unions and employers, rather like an industrial tribunal in the United Kingdom. Others thought that the proposal did not go far enough—it would not solve the "overload" problem. Other types of case should be given to the new court as well as staff cases.

After many years of discussion, the new Court of First Instance or *Tribunal de Première instance* was created.[1] To avoid confusion between the Courts and equally to avoid repetition of the full English title and the current passion for acronyms, I refer to the Court of First Instance by its French designation, *le Tribunal*, anglicised to the Tribunal. The Tribunal has 12 judges,[2] one from each Member State, and is likely and indeed is intended to sit principally in chambers of three or five judges, rather than in banc. Perhaps 12 judges, for political reasons, were inevitable though the Court felt that as a start it was enough to have seven judges, to allow two chambers of three and an extra judge to allow for the duties of the President, for absences, and for occasional free periods of research.

"Twelve or seven?" at one stage seemed an issue, but in the long run it does not matter if the Tribunal sits in chambers, and 12 will certainly be needed if the Tribunal is to have more than the staff cases, competition cases and cases under the European Coal and Steel Treaty which are sent to it at present. The 12 members are all judges, one in fact from each Member State. There are no separate advocates general as there are in the Court, but for particular cases—those involving substantial factual investigation—one judge can be nominated to carry out the functions of an advocate general.

It seems clear at present that if the Court has had too much to do—as I think it has though others say that internal procedural changes could speed up or make

---

[1] *Cf.* Article 168A, inserted into the Treaty by Article 11 of the Single European Act.
[2] *Cf.* Council Decision 88/591 of October 24, 1988 establishing a Court of First Instance, O.J. (1988) L.319.

efficient the working of the Court—the Tribunal, until recently, has certainly not had too much to do. The disproportion seems likely to get worse rather than better if things are left as they are since there are now far fewer cases involving steel quotas and other issues under the European Coal and Steel Treaty than there were a few years ago. Conversely, where questions arise in new areas of Community activity (as for example under the directives dealing with the internal market, with social policy, with the environment, with telecommunications, with training), they must under present arrangements all go to the Court.

In theoretical terms the solution is simple—transfer some of the Court's jurisdiction to the Tribunal. Clearly, however, any redistribution of work should not be worked out merely on a quantitative basis. It must be worked out on a rational and practical basis, choosing the right forum for each category of case. In concrete terms the solution is not at all simple: to every possibility there seems to be an objection. Thus, by way of example, the anti-dumping cases[3] and the State aids cases can involve extensive factual investigations—akin to the competition cases—and seem just the material for the Tribunal. They are all relevant to the removal of anti-competitive practices from the Community. The objection sometimes heard as to both of these categories being transferred is that the Court has not yet had enough cases to enable it to develop principles and guidelines so that a transfer of jurisdiction should wait until it has. In any event, on State aids, some Member States may prefer that these cases should stay with the Court in view of their importance in legal and financial terms.

---

[3] By Article 3 of the Decision establishing the Court of First Instance, the Member States agreed to reconsider jurisdiction in anti-dumping cases two years after the Court of First Instance began work.

It also seems unlikely that Member States would agree, at this stage, that any proceedings by or against Member States or the institutions should go direct to the Tribunal. That possibility may, however, have to be faced one day. The State aids cases are very much part of the "competition" family of cases, which in part do go to the Tribunal. The reports for the hearing and the judgments in two recent cases brought by Italy show that much detail can be involved.[4] This should be dealt with by the Tribunal. Where an important general question of law lies at the heart of such cases it can be dealt with on appeal.

A second possibility might be to transfer other cases, less sensitive than the State aids cases, where detailed investigation of facts is necessary. Quickly come to mind the so-called "FEOGA" cases where disputes arise between the Commission and Member States as to whether, for example, subsidies paid to farmers or wine makers are recoverable from the Community or whether they have been paid otherwise than in conformity with Community rules.[5] Here, too, there is a problem since such cases can involve important questions of interpretation which seem likely to reach the Court in any event by way of appeal. Moreover, once again substantial financial interests of the Member States are involved and the relationship between the liabilities of the institutions and the Member States is at issue.

Other cases, which can sometimes involve complex questions of mixed fact and law, arise in social security and customs matters (that is, customs duties on goods coming for the first time into the Community, since customs duties on goods passing from one Member State

---

[4] Case 303/88 *Italy* v. *Commission* and Case 305/89 *Italy* v. *Commission*, both judgments March 21, 1991, not yet reported.
[5] See, for example, Case C–22/90 *France* v. *Commission*, judgment of November 7, 1991, not yet reported.

to another have been abolished). These, however, more frequently arise on references from national courts under Article 177 of the Treaty.

Theoretically, it would be possible to decide that certain classes of case referred under Article 177 should be sent to the Tribunal. Alternatively, it would not be impossible in practice to give the Court the power to send to the Tribunal all cases which the Court considered did not need to be dealt with at first instance by the Court. If there were a right of appeal, even if subject to the grant of leave, then cases could go finally to the Court if it were found that the point of law was more important or more difficult than the Court had first thought, or if the Tribunal were felt by the parties, the Member States or the institutions to have gone wrong in a way which justified an appeal.

On the other hand, there are structural as well as conceptual difficulties involved in allowing an appeal on a reference from a national court. Even more fundamentally, to any transfer of preliminary questions it can be objected that this would interfere with the special relationship which has been built up between the Court and national judges over the years. The Court goes to great lengths not to trespass on the functions of the national judge (that is, to decide national law, to consider specific national legislation in the light of Community law or to decide the case before the national judge) and in return the national judge by and large loyally accepts and applies the rulings of the Court. National judges, it might be said, want the ruling of the Court and not that of a first instance court. Particularly might this be objected to where questions are sent and answers have to be complied with by courts of final resort. This objection, in my view, can be exaggerated and may become less forceful as the Tribunal gains in experience and stature. It has, however, a certain validity.

Perhaps, in practical terms, an equally serious risk would be that there would be inconsistency of decisions between the Court and the Tribunal if no appeal procedure were provided, or even with such procedure, if in a particular case there were no appeal.

There are other objections to sending Article 177 references to the Tribunal. First, it is not necessarily clear at an early stage which cases will, in the end, raise a serious question so that, on a first investigation, the wrong cases could be sent or retained. Secondly, not many of these cases, except perhaps where the validity of the act of an institution is under review, raise factual issues of the kind which it was originally intended should go to the Tribunal.

In addition, there is no doubt that it is difficult to find acceptable ways of dividing up the questions. Apart from the problems already mentioned, it seems that to separate cases on validity from cases on interpretation is not acceptable, since both can raise questions of importance and difficulty. Nor is it sufficient to decide simply on the basis that references from a final court go to the Court, whereas others go to the Tribunal, since questions from courts of first instance or at whatever level on an intermediate appeal can raise questions of supreme importance. One has only to remember *Costa* v. *ENEL*,[6] which came from a magistrate and which decided that Community law overrode national law, to realise this.

Yet a further possibility would be to require to be sent to the Tribunal all cases begun by natural and legal persons under the second paragraph of Article 173 (claims that a decision, addressed to, or of direct and individual concern to, the applicant, even if addressed to

[6] Case 6/64 [1964] E.C.R. 1141.

another or in the form of a regulation, is illegal on the ground of lack of competence or infringement of the Treaty), or under the second paragraph of Article 175 (claims that an institution of the Community has failed to address to the applicant an act after having been called upon to do so and having failed to define its position). Such a course would have the advantage that the category is clearly defined and does not depend on a subjective assessment or the exercise of a discretion. In addition, such cases can, though they do not always, involve an investigation of detail. On the other hand, they are relatively few in number, since the test for admission is strictly applied, so that to transfer them would not greatly reduce the workload of the Court. Moreover, since people and trading companies already form an "unprivileged" class for the purposes of actions for annulment, it might be seen as limiting their status further by excluding them from the Court and requiring them to begin in the Tribunal—a factor which would not be cured by even an automatic right of appeal. However, this might be a suitable category of cases to send to the Tribunal and give, from the administrative point of view, a clear dividing line. The fact that there may be an overlap between issues raised in an Article 177 reference (the Court) and a direct action (the Tribunal) could clearly lead to difficulties of conflict or, at any rate, of coincidence of jurisdiction which would need to be resolved but at this stage they do not seem insuperable.

These possibilities merely illustrate the difficulties of finding an acceptable way of giving the Court a more manageable workload. I am convinced that the problem will, unless ameliorations can be devised, become more acute. In time, as Community rules interlace more and more with national rules, the task of the Court will increase. Then, an enlargement of the Court, a larger or a second Tribunal, may have to be considered. It is not difficult to envisage an arrangement under which decisions of national courts or administrative agencies on specified matters (for example, customs classifications) should go direct by way of a challenge to the Tribunal rather than by way of an Article 177 reference. I do not, however, believe that the time is ripe for regional courts, albeit subject to a right of appeal to the Court, or that this is, at present, the best course to adopt. It may, however, have to be considered later. If—or, as I think, as—Europe becomes more integrated, however slowly and surefootedly this ought to be, and as new Member States accede to the Community, the case for a parallel court structure alongside the national, or in United States terms the state, court structure will become stronger. It may become more needed: it may become theoretically more defensible.

It also has to be borne in mind that the practical effects of the creation of the Tribunal have not yet fully been seen. A flood of competition cases would give much work to the Tribunal thereby reducing what would otherwise have been the Court's case load. Perhaps more important, it is not yet known in what percentage of the cases, or in how many cases, the parties will seek to appeal. That could make a substantial addition to the Court's workload and initially there will be many difficult procedural and substantive questions to resolve until the appeals system is fully developed. What is "fact" and what is "law" is an early tease, which can probably only be worked out wisely on a case-by-case basis.

Many of the staff cases seem likely to be resolved by decisions on fact—whatever the difference between fact and law accepted by the Court. Again, whilst it seemed to me initially that in the Article 85 or Article 86 cases an appeal was likely in most if not all of them, if there was an arguable point of law, it may be that the parties will in some cases be satisfied with a partial decision in their favour, whether as to the substance or as to the fine imposed. If the fine is reduced that is enough. The legal issue can wait for another case.

For the moment a centralised court and tribunal or tribunals seem to me sufficient, such as tribunals of specialised jurisdictions, as for patents or trade marks, or of a limited but more generalised jurisdiction like the present Tribunal. What, however, is essential both under the present system and under an alternative system with more tribunals or a parallel structure of Community courts, is that the Court of Justice should be the final arbiter of questions of law. To create rival "final courts" with conflicting decisions and doubts as to the determination of jurisdictions can only lead to chaos. It would gravely harm the development of the *acquis communautaire* on consistent lines. Suggestions heard, if only by way of gossip, that there should be a special constitutional court to deal with issues of "subsidiary" or to deal with intellectual property matters seem to me likely to cause great mischief. Where rules have to be spelled out, even hammered out in the teeth of opposition by Member States, it is safer to leave the final word to one set of judges rather than to leave it in the hands of several sets. I repeat that there can, in my view, only be one Supreme Court.

Whatever should be done does not, however, depend on the decision of the Court. It is for the Member States to decide. In the Single European Act the Member States gave power to the Council, acting unanimously, to set up a Tribunal having jurisdiction to determine at first instance "certain classes of action or proceedings brought by natural legal persons." It is clear from what has been said that only a very limited number of classes of action or proceedings have so far been transferred. The Council, thus, seems to have power, without further

Treaty amendment, to transfer other classes brought by natural or legal persons. To do that may be the first step. If more is to be done it may need a Treaty amendment specifying the jurisdiction of the Tribunal or giving to the Council power to transfer other classes of proceedings without Treaty amendment. The latter has the advantage that it can be done more easily and simply if the Member States agree. The former seems clearly preferable since a change in the jurisdiction of the Court would be involved. Such a constitutional alteration should, in principle, be incorporated into the Treaty itself.

Taking away some categories of case is not, however, the only solution. There are, in my view, other matters to be considered. Their solution could increase the efficiency of the Court and reduce the workload of its members, though I accept that subjective personal opinions affect one's thinking as to whether there exists a problem and, if so, how it can be solved. Some or all of my colleagues in the Court may disagree with everything I say. In this lecture I can only give examples—others may readily think of better ones to resolve the problem.

In the first place it seems to me that in some ways our procedures could, for particular purposes, be altered, whether by the Court or if necessary by the Council, or even the Member States. There is a rigidity of procedure which could be relaxed by rule. Thus, if an action is brought by the Commission under Article 169 of the Treaty for a declaration that a Member State is in breach of its Treaty obligations, there may be a serious issue to be tried. Is a rule or practice under national law contrary to a clear principle of Community law in that it is discriminatory or disproportionate? Has a Member State sufficiently implemented a directive when it has purported to do so? In such cases the panoply of the Court's procedures is justified: written claim, defence, reply, rejoinder; report for the hearing; oral argument with two speeches for each party and questions; advocate general's opinion; written judgment following deliberation, which can be long; report in the law reports.

Yet, sometimes quite frequently, there is not, and is not asserted to be, any answer to the Commission's claim. All that is said by the Member State is that the national measure will soon be adopted: "The Minister has been busy"; "The Parliament was dissolved just as it was about to be passed"; "Our procedures are very complicated." In these, and in equally clear cases under Article 169, there should be a procedure for an order declaring the breach, or for judgment "by consent" or "in default." Member States do not lose in dignity by admitting that they have failed to adopt legislation and by facing the music. By so doing they would save themselves, the Commission and the Court much time, and the taxpayer much expense. Conversely, to drag out the procedures where there is a semblance of an argument, then to adopt satisfactory legislation but to ask the Court not to make any order, or to try to shame the Commission into withdrawing its claim, because finally by the date of the hearing there has been a compliance, seems to me regrettably time-wasting. Fortunately, under rules adopted this year, the Court can, from September 1991, with the express consent of the parties, dispense with an oral hearing in direct actions.[7] In respect of preliminary rulings, the parties in the main action, the Member States, the Commission and, where appropriate, the Council, are asked whether they wish to present oral argument. In the absence of a positive response the Court may decide to dispense with

---

[7] Article 44(a) of the Rules of Procedure of the Court of Justice of the European Communities of June 19, 1991, O.J. (1991) L.176, p. 7.

a hearing.[8] In appeals, the Court may decide to dispense with a hearing unless one of the parties objects on the ground that the written procedure did not enable him fully to defend his point of view.[9] In the sort of cases to which I referred previously, the Commission and the Member State may be expected to agree to dispense with the oral hearing, though they may not in every case. I am not satisfied, however, that more could not be done to reduce the length of such cases.

The practice is different where a Member State not only fails to implement a directive but also fails to give effect to a judgment declaring it to be in breach for not having done so. Then I think there is something to be said for beating a disapproving drum and the hearing gives a chance to the Court to do so.

Answering references under Article 177 of the Treaty is as important as any of the Court's functions and has clearly provided a means for developing bedrock principles of Community law. The Court should be slow to refuse to deal with these questions or to curtail their scope.[10] Even so, unnecessary duplications should be avoided since, once the case is registered, unless it is withdrawn, the full procedure has to be gone through. If, as has happened on a number of occasions, the identical question—identical in form and substance— has been referred, I have long thought that the Court should have the power by order to reiterate its reply to the previous question, if the national judge would not or could not withdraw his question once the earlier decision was drawn to his attention.

This line of thinking is reflected in a change now introduced as Article 104(3) of the Rules of Procedure. If

[8] Article 104(4) of the Rules of Procedure.
[9] Article 120 of the Rules of Procedure.
[10] See my opinion in *Foglia* v. *Novello No. 2* (Case 244/80 [1981] E.C.R. 3945 at 3069).

the Court finds that a question referred is "manifestly identical to a question on which the Court has already ruled," then, after informing the referring court and considering any observations submitted to it by the parties to the case, the Member States, the Commission and, in some circumstances, the Council, and after hearing the advocate general, the Court may "give its decision by reasoned order in which reference is made to its previous judgment." Here, too, oral argument may be dispensed with provided that none of the persons involved has asked for the opportunity to present oral argument.

I do not see any real danger in giving the Court this power. It is highly improbable that the Court will abuse it so as to refuse references where there really was a difference between the questions referred. If a judge thinks that a second case raises a different issue he can frame the question differently from that in the first case. If he thinks that the question is the same but that the circumstances have changed, or that some significant argument had not been put forward in the first case, he can spell it out in the order for reference and the Court would clearly take account of it. It is necessary to ensure that Member States and the Commission are notified of the Court's intention to reject a reference (on the basis that the question is identical to one previously asked) so that, if they had missed it the first time or thought that the two questions were not identical, they could intervene in the second case. If the national judge is dissatisfied by the rejection, he can make a further order for reference explaining why the two are not the same. Subject to these safeguards in an admittedly limited number of cases, time, it seems, can be saved.

Some anxiety is now felt about an increasing failure by Member States to comply with judgments of the Court. This is a relatively new phenomenon in terms of scale.

There were, in the past, occasions when Member States did not put right a breach declared after Article 169 proceedings. Usually, however, they did it after a second application was made. For judges to fail, or to refuse, to follow a ruling of the Court was happily even more rare. Although the number of cases where Member States have failed to comply with a judgment of the Court is, in the middle of 1991, almost 60, I am not satisfied that there is yet cause for panic on the basis that the rule of law is at risk, regrettable though such failures are.

On an Article 169 application, the Court has no jurisdiction except to make a declaration of breach and it does not normally specify what has to be done to remedy the breach. It has no power to enforce its order or to punish for the breach—no tipstaff, no Tower of London, no sequestration.

There have been proposals that some enforcement powers should be provided. One suggestion was that the Court should be empowered to fine for a failure to comply with a judgment. Whether it was desirable that the Court should be involved in assessing degrees of guilt and the consequences of guilt seemed to be debatable. A variation on this idea was that enforcement powers should be vested in the Commission, as in the European Coal and Steel Community Treaty, but subject to review by the Court. If it were thought right to give the Commission the power to fine, that could be reviewed—just as the Court has power to review fines for breaches of Articles 85 and 86 of the Treaty.

However, it appears now to be accepted generally that the Court should have the power to fine for such failure.

The other suggestion was that individuals, including companies, should be given, by the Treaty, the right to compensation for damage caused by a Member State's failure to implement Community obligations, for example, by failing to give effect to a directive. It seemed desirable, if this were to be done, that the liability and the assessment of damages should follow Community rules rather than vary according to the national rules of Member States. That could, no doubt, be done without too much difficulty in respect of liability—was negligence or wilful failure or fraud a necessary or sufficient element? More difficult might be the statement of Community guidelines as to the quantum of damages. If such claims had to be brought before the Court or the Tribunal that might not matter too much since a consistent coherent set of rules could be decided on by the judges. Because of their likely number, the Court itself could certainly not deal with such cases: whether they would be likely to submerge the Tribunal is difficult to forecast. On the other hand, national judges could no doubt cope with the volume of cases but, if the claims had to be brought in national courts, clear guidelines in the interests of a consistent coherent code of damages would be essential.

This proposal, however, needs to be considered in the light of, and may have been superseded by, recent judgments. A Member State can already get itself into a terrible muddle if it fails to transpose a directive (the most common subject-matter of Article 169 proceedings). For example, in a line of recent cases which came before the Court by way of references for a preliminary ruling from the High Court and the Supreme Court of Ireland,[11] a Member State succeeded in making matters worse for itself by reason of its own failure to transpose a directive in good time. Ireland failed fully to transpose

---

[11] Case 286/85 *Cotter and McDermott* v. *Minister for Social Welfare and Attorney General* [1987] E.C.R. 1453, Case 377/89 *Cotter and McDermott* v. *Minister for Social Welfare and Attorney General*, judgment of March 13, 1991, not yet reported, and Case 208/90 *Emmott* v. *Minister for Social Welfare and Attorney General*, judgment of July 25, 1991, not yet reported.

the directive on equality of treatment in social security matters[12] and maintained on its statute books provisions whereby married men seeking social security benefits were treated more favourably than married women in identical situations. The Court held that the Member State was obliged to grant married women the same benefits as married men in identical circumstances. This had the effect that, for the period between the date when the directive should have been transposed and the date when it was in fact transposed, married women were entitled to the more favourable rate of benefit applying to married men. This was despite the fact that when the Member State ultimately transposed the directive, it ensured equality of treatment partially by levelling down the level of benefit payable to married men and partially by levelling up the level payable to married women. It would therefore have been cheaper for the Member State to have transposed the directive in good time.

In *Emmott*, the third of this line of cases, the Court held that if an individual brings proceedings before national courts in order to protect rights directly conferred by a directive, the Member State may not rely on its own domestic limitation period so long as the Member State has not properly transposed the directive into its domestic legal system.

We can see from this that if a Member State has failed to transpose a directive which the Court holds to be directly effective, the interpretation of national and Community law is such that the Member State will not be able to escape the obligations flowing therefrom. Even if the Court holds that the directive is not directly effective, in the light of the recent judgment in *Francovich*

---

[12] Council Directive 79/7/EEC, on the progressive implementation of equal treatment for men and women in matters of social security, O.J. (1979) L.6, p. 24.

and Bonifaci to which I have already referred,[13] the Member State will now be obliged to provide compensation for damage caused to an individual by the Member State's failure to transpose the directive on time. This case is obviously of enormous importance and its practical implications will no doubt be worked out in subsequent references to the Court. However, in conjunction with the doctrine of direct effect, the case will help to ensure that a Member State is obliged, on the domestic plane, to make good any financial loss caused to individuals by its failure to transpose a directive properly. It may well be that this principle will be more effective in encouraging Member States to transpose directives on time than a system of monetary penalties would be.

In the interests of speed and efficiency, other matters will, from time to time, need to be discussed. We have, for example, a practice of trying to give precedence to Article 177 references in preparing reports for the hearing and in fixing dates. Perhaps the Court needs a more formalised "fast track" procedure for these references and for appeals from the Tribunal, once we see sufficiently clearly the procedures these should follow and establish our own guidelines.

We have limited oral argument. I was not persuaded that rules limiting argument to 15 and 30 minutes were necessary (an experienced presiding judge can stop irrelevant and verbose speeches) particularly as the substance of cases before the Chambers and the Court varies very much. Moreover, some lawyers have to come a long way to Luxembourg. Fifteen minutes for someone coming from Athens, Sicily, Granada or Shannon seems a bit restrictive. It has, however, worked reasonably well. If a lawyer asks for more time on good grounds, he

---

[13] Joined Cases C–6 and C–9/90, judgment of November 19, 1991, not yet reported.

is likely to get *some* more time. If he has a good point
which he puts well, he may be allowed to continue
beyond the limit. He can make up a lot of ground in
answering questions and in his reply, if he is skilful.
Moreover, English and Irish lawyers appearing before
the Court have been surprised, once they have accepted
the discipline, at how much they can pack incisively into
30 minutes, sometimes with advantage, compared with
an unlimited, rather general, address. Maybe, without
losing the immense value of the debate between Bar and
Bench which occurs in the United Kingdom (but which
does not exist in the Court), there are some lessons to be
learned in national appellate courts from a reasonable
time limitation.

If there is something for the United Kingdom courts to
learn about regulating oral hearings, there is a great deal
for the Court to learn from United Kingdom practice
about the written and documentary preparation and
presentation of a case. The written pleadings, necessarily
longer because they must set out all the grounds for an
application or of a defence, together with the supporting
arguments, tend to become longer than in the past,
particularly in the reply and the rejoinder. I think we
may have to find a way of discouraging this. No less
unsatisfactory in a heavy case is the way of presenting
documents to the Court. They are appended to the
pleadings in the order in which they are referred to,
which has a certain sense, but with four or more
pleadings, especially if there are interventions, it is not
easy for the Court to find a way through the exhibits
whether chronologically, by subject or otherwise. I hope
that the Tribunal will do what we have failed to do,
despite pleas to the contrary, and will insist, in heavy
cases, that bundles are prepared in some sort of order.

I used to think—the common lawyer reacting to the
civil law system—that the form of written pleadings was

unnecessarily rigid, but the method is now long established and reasonably well understood throughout the Community, and United Kingdom and Irish lawyers will have to adjust to it. Many of them have already done so. Translating or even defining terms in the Rules of Procedure, however, is not always easy, especially for lawyers not accustomed to the formalities of French pleadings as adopted at the Court. To tell the English lawyer that he must set out separately his *moyens* each backed by all the *arguments* and leading to his final *conclusions* does not tell him much. It may say more to the Scottish lawyer. The borderline between *moyen* and *argument* does not at first seem clear and *conclusions* sounds a bit vague—no more than a final and maybe flowery peroration.

We finally settled, in the Rules of Procedure, on "grounds" to represent *moyens*; "pleas in law" would have been more poetic and comfortable for the Scots though less familiar, at any rate in recent times, to the English and Irish lawyers. *Conclusions* could have been used as an English word particularly as it has long been used in the "Reports of cases before the Court" in English but it is subject to misinterpretation, not least since the advocate general also gives his "opinion" under the French heading *conclusions*. Moreover, in the English rules relating to both the Court and the Tribunal: "The conclusions reached by the majority of the judges after final discussion shall determine the decision of the Court. . . . "[14] So, in the end, it seemed wiser and clearer to resort to "the form of order sought" rather than conclusions.

If we can effectively reduce, without stultifying, the oral proceedings, and if we can limit and keep in manageable form the written pleadings, then the

[14] Article 27(5) Court, Article 33(5) Tribunal.

question arises whether the Court can do anything with its own procedures to reduce delay and increase efficiency.

Each case, as it comes in, is assigned to a judge reporter (for some reason referred to in English as the judge *rapporteur*) and to an advocate general. There is no doubt that there is some duplication in the work they each do. They both go through the documents in depth at an early stage and generally agree the preliminary report to the whole Court of 19 members as to what the future procedure should be. They both prepare a statement as to what the result should be—one as an opinion and the other as a draft of reasons. When we were becoming overloaded and there seemed to be no progress towards a Tribunal, I used to think that a possible solution would be to convert the advocates general into additional judges, either generally or ad hoc. That, at any rate, would have given two more chambers of three judges or one of five judges. Now we have the Tribunal and such a radical solution, it was thought, would not be needed. Even so it may be worth considering, in the light of the Tribunal's experience, whether the Court could follow the new procedure of the Tribunal by appointing one of its members ad hoc to fulfil the role of an advocate general. As an advocate general, one always hoped that the function had some utility; as a judge I now know that it is very valuable in this kind of court to have a detailed first-round assessment on which the judges can work. The research, the analysis of fact and law, the direction indicated by the advocate general—even if not followed—are of considerable help. I still think that there are some cases where a formal, written opinion of the advocate general is not necessary—cases of uncontested failure by a Member State to fulfil its obligations, if they are to continue in their present form, merit no more than an extempore oral statement to the effect that the Commission has established the breach in the terms of the form of order sought.

If the written pleadings are at the core of the presentation of a case, the délibéré is the place where the judgment is hammered out. Without breaching its confidentiality, I may say that this can be an absorbing and a highly creative experience. The search for agreement on principles, the detailed examination of ideas and language, can reach a very high level. Starting from very different professional and cultural backgrounds, we all arrive with certain predispositions, even prejudices, of which we may or may not be consciously aware. Getting through these to achieve a consensus or a decision on points which should be seen as distinct from, even if eventually they are to form part of, our own national laws and legal systems is not always easy. A good aspect of the délibéré of the full Court is that A may strongly ally with B in one case or on one issue but no less strongly oppose him in the next. "Talking it out" can sometimes be a very creative and indeed impressive experience.

Despite all the merits of the délibéré, and accepting that it is inevitable that there should be oral discussion of both the principle and the detail of a decision in order to explore all the issues and to find at least a consensus in a way which is not necessary if separate judgments can be given, it seems to me that the Court should from time to time ask itself whether its discussions need be so long. A certain self-discipline would be good for each of us and more time for individual work would enure to the benefit of the Court. This is no less true (by which I mean it is infinitely more true) of the administrative discussions of the Court. There are matters which justify the decision of all 19 members of the Court. There are others which quite plainly do not—and it is not unusual amongst lawyers in committee (as no doubt with other councils) for the trivial items to occupy a disproportionate time. It is said that the governing body of one professional institution in London spent more hours discussing whether they should wear a white or a black tie at the annual dinner than they spent on issues of principle. The university departmental meeting in Malcolm Bradbury's *The History Man* is another example of the same phenomenon, this time in an academic context.[15] I think that sometimes we tend to behave in the same way. I am often tempted to carry into the meeting a copy of Patrick Leigh Fermor's *A time to keep silence*[16] as a reminder!

Far more of the administration should be delegated to a committee; far more of the administration conducted personally by the President and his chambers should (as it seems from outside those chambers) be conducted by others. The burden on the President, who must add to his responsibility of leading a team, chairing meetings, representing the Court externally, having a wide vision as to the development of the law and the trends which the Court is taking, the responsibility for so much detailed administration, is very heavy. We have had a succession of dedicated Presidents including in the front rank of dedication the present incumbent. At some time, in some way, there must be some delegation, if only for the protection of the President.

But to return to the deliberation, it seems to me necessary, for the Court to proceed with reasonable dispatch, that finicky ("fussy" as one of my colleagues would describe it) drafting changes should be avoided-even though this may sometimes be frustrating for the francophones. We could well emulate more of the

[15] Secker and Warburg (1975), London.
[16] John Murray (Publishers), (1957, 1982), London.

practice of the United States Supreme Court in exchanging notes and I have the impression that amongst many if not all members of the Court a written procedure of discussion is increasingly approved. The questions emerge more precisely. If done in good time before an oral discussion, with consequent time for reflection, this enables the discussion to be more pointed and usually much briefer.

There is, of course, a fundamental difference in our procedures which distinguishes us from the Supreme Court of the United States, a difference reflected in the length of time we take over the délibéré and the final drafting of a judgment. The Court gives one judgment which everybody who sits on the case signs.

This partly explains not only the style—as often as possible following well-trodden paths, using formulae which have by now a well-established meaning, tenaciously believing that to change the word changes the sense—but also the content, since frequently the draft seeks to accommodate nuances separating those on the same side, pacifying those who disagree. There is no doubt that practising lawyers and national judges do not always find the judgments clear or readily intelligible. I know from experience as both. I think, however, that a degree of formalism is inevitable, perhaps accentuated by the fact that all judgments are drafted in one language which inevitably is not the first language of most members of the Court. There is an inbuilt tendency to play safe and to follow the pattern. On the other hand, in my view, there is room for some flexibility of style and some of the jargon could with advantage disappear. Although it is necessary to have some "joining phrases" and to distinguish between recitation of argument and the Court's own views, an automatic scattering of *"il convient de," "il y a lieu de relever," "il y a lieu de constater"* could well be avoided. Even without going as far as Lord Denning's opening sentence, "It was bluebell time in Kent,"[17] a little freshness of style and individuality need not detract from the clarity. It would certainly add to the ease of reading some of the judgments. It will be interesting to see how the style of the Tribunal's judgments develops—with no report for the hearing, they are fuller and, so far, seem to me to be very readable, if they do not become too long.

A more relaxed personal style would, of course, be easier if individual judgments were given. Even if there were one majority and one minority judgment there could be greater strength and clarity of expression since there would be less need to accommodate compromise. I am not conscious that this question has really been thought out in recent times, if ever. Collegiate, anonymous opinions were the order of the day in the original Member States and there is a tendency to assume now that that must be so and always will be so. I do not accept either assumption. It was, in my view, right to begin with one collegiate judgment—the Supreme Court of the United States had no dissenting judgments for the first 35 or so years. For a court, however, which, even if still very young, is well established, it is not in my opinion a sign of weakness or a necessary source of confusion to allow dissent. If judges upholding one view can say so strongly, that may give a clearer judgment. Those who dissent may well aid the subsequent development of the Court's jurisprudence and it should not be feared that they will necessarily want to ride their own hobby horses. I feel, without knowing, that at present there would be little, if any, support for a proposal to allow dissenting judgments, though I equally feel, without knowing, that other judges as well as I may occasionally wish that they could make it clear that they

[17] *Hinz* v. *Berry* (C.A.) [1970] 2 Q.B. 41.

do not subscribe to a ruling on the law which they find particularly objectionable. If the tenure of judges becomes more secure (mandates of six years, renewal being dependent on political change, even on political "arrangements," being not very secure) then dissenting opinions might be more acceptable. This proposal, however, despite the speed of modern change, is probably for the next and not for this century.

For this century there is already much to think about—not just internally but as to the Court's position in relation actually to the Tribunal and potentially, or at any rate possibly, to disputes which may have to be resolved in the "European Economic Area," or in relation to newly-admitted members or "affiliates."[18]

The Tribunal is "attached to the Court" and is not a separate institution; to some extent they share facilities —administration, research, the library—and this sharing need cause no insuperable problems. There were bound to be areas where the precise relationship of the Court and the Tribunal had to be worked out—the budget, approaches to the other institutions on matters of concern to one or both, even protocol which, in a multinational, like an international, organisation never seems quite to disappear from sight. These problems will resolve themselves if they have not already done so. On the personal level, there already exists a good relationship with individual members of the Tribunal. It was evidenced very clearly on the day when five of us (two from the Court and three from the Tribunal) sat to judge the final of the European Moot Court Competition. Even though we took the Moot very seriously, it was for the five of us a very agreeable, even jolly, day and none of the others in the least minded that out of 60 or 70

[18] *The Independent*, July 24, 1991.

teams, representing most of the Member States, Gray's Inn was the obvious final winner!

On the jurisdictional side there are other matters to be sorted out. These are inherent in the creation of an appeal system—and for the first time the Court now exercises an appellate jurisdiction. Thus, the Court had to work out in practice the form of reports for the hearing, ordonnances and judgments on appeal. How should we distinguish between fact and law to know whether an appeal was manifestly inadmissible as not raising an issue of law? How far should we regard an inference from primary facts as a question of law which could be reviewed on appeal? How liberal or how tough should we be in the early days in dealing with the question whether an appeal was manifestly unfounded? What is the content of the various grounds of appeal: "lack of competence"; "breach of procedure which can be shown 'adversely to affect the interests of the appellant' "; "infringement of Community law?"[19]

Where an appeal is brought against a decision of the Tribunal, Article 52 of the Statute of the Court provides that the procedure shall consist of a written part and an oral part: "In accordance with conditions laid down in the Rules of Procedure, the Court of Justice, having heard the Advocate General and the parties, may dispense with the oral part." It seemed likely that some appeals could be dealt with fairly without an oral hearing. If the parties consented (and from continental countries their lawyers might be well disposed to do so) then there would be no problem, unless the Court itself wanted oral argument. But what if the parties or one of them wanted an oral hearing and the other did not?

---

[19] Article 51 of the Statute of the Court of Justice of the European Communities, added by Article 7 of the Council Decision establishing a Court of First Instance (see note 2).

The common lawyer would probably favour an extensive right to an oral hearing, the civil lawyer would probably retain a wide discretion to the Court to refuse it. In the end a curious compromise was reached. On the close of written pleadings the Court may, on report of the judge reporter, having heard the advocate general and the parties, decide to dispense with the oral procedure, unless one of the parties objects on the ground that the written procedure did not enable him fully to defend his point of view. Does this mean that a mere objection that the written procedure did not enable a party to defend his point of view entitles him to an oral hearing or does the Court decide whether the objection is made out? In what circumstances can it be said (and how far will counsel want to assert or confess) that the written procedure did not enable the party fully to defend his point of view? Whatever use is made of this proviso, it seems clear that the Court has a discretion and it seems likely that the Court will exercise it in favour of the applicant where a reasonable justification can be put forward for an oral hearing. In any case, the discretion has to be exercised *against* an oral hearing ("to dispense with" it) rather than in *favour* of an oral hearing, the balance thus, if anything, being loaded in favour of the applicant. Hearts may harden later but it is not impossible that in the early days the Court will be reluctant to refuse a hearing in a case which is only just not "clearly inadmissible or clearly unfounded."

The effect of an appellate judgment on the Tribunal has caused some debate amongst lawyers—and that vigorously at the excellent conference organised by David Vaughan Q.C. and the Union Internationale des Avocats together with the Danish Bar in Copenhagen. By Article 54 of the Statute of the Court, where a case is referred back to the Tribunal, the latter "shall be bound

by the decision of the Court of Justice on points of law.''
That Article does not apply to matters of fact since the
appeal to the Court is limited to points of law.[20] It
clearly means that in the case in question the Tribunal
must apply the law as decided by the Court in that case.
But what of other cases which follow? Is the Tribunal
bound to apply that statement of the law in later cases,
either as a matter of the interpretation of the rule or as a
principle of Community law? I have heard it argued
strongly that it does not and that the Tribunal is free
later to say that in another case the law is different. The
question is parallel to, but obviously not the same as,
that which used to be discussed in connection with the
Court's answers to references under Article 177 of the
Treaty. Even if all judges dealing with the case involved
in the reference are bound to apply the law on
interpretation or validity as declared by the Court on
such a reference, are judges in other cases also bound?

The effect of a decision on an appeal in relation to
later cases is a matter for decision by the Court but in
my view, since the Court is the appellate court, the
Tribunal must apply the law as declared by the Court in
an earlier case. Thus the Tribunal may be able to
distinguish the decision in different situations but, if the
later case is on all fours with the former, the Tribunal
must apply the law as declared even if it says: ''But for
the Court's decision we should have decided differently
for the following reasons . . . ,'' and then leaves it to the
Court on appeal to reconsider the question.

This is by no means an academic question. The judge
in the national court may have to decide, if the Tribunal
is free to take a different decision from the Court in a
later case, whether he applies the law declared by the

---

[20] Article 51.

Court (as the higher court) or the Tribunal (as the court giving the later decision).

One of the criticisms of the Court by lawyers and their clients—some Japanese in-house lawyers at a conference upbraided me severely over this—is that the Court does not go into the facts sufficiently when reviewing competition and anti-dumping cases. There were two reasons for this—one legal, that the Court regarded such investigations as being outside the scope of judicial review under Article 173 of the Treaty—the other pragmatic, in that the Court simply did not have time to do so. No less has the Court been criticised by American lawyers for failing to make any economic or commercial appreciation of the issues decided by the Commission. This inquiry again can be said to a large extent to fall outside judicial review and is perhaps not very wise until we have a generation of judges who are also economists! If Professor Whish's book on Competition Law[21] has its way, that may come about, astonishing though it might have seemed to some of the generations of national judges before mine. The Tribunal will no doubt be urged to go more into the evidence, to see whether the evidence overall really justifies a Commission finding rather than merely to see whether there is manifest error. It is interesting to note that the first major hearing in a competition case before the Tribunal was listed for six days, the Tribunal being prepared to sit from 9.30 am until 7.00 pm including, if necessary, Saturday. The suggestion of a hearing lasting more than a day in the Court causes eruptions. Perhaps this indicates a different approach. What the Court will say on appeal about the limits of judicial review if the Tribunal does go further into the facts or into economic "second guessing" of the Commission remains to be

---

[21] Richard Whish, *Competition Law*, (Butterworths, 1989, London).

seen. I am very conscious of what the lawyers of the parties other than the Commission think about it.

We are now facing the possibility of great developments in the Community.

In the first place, the legislation bringing into play the Single Market—abolishing physical, fiscal and technical barriers to trade—will no doubt provide a plethora of cases for the Court: references from national courts, direct challenges to validity, allegations of non-compliance by Member States. The range of measures is already very extensive and there are more to come. Directives on public procurement, technical harmonisation over a wide field (with a new approach defining the essential requirements which a product has to meet rather than spelling out the details), capital movements, banking, insurance company law, taxation, transport, telecommunications and intellectual property, to name only some, have already been adopted.

For the Court there will be major issues beyond the interpretation of these directives. Questions seem likely to arise as to whether particular directives were made under the right article of the Treaty and whether proper procedures were followed; whether the co-operation procedure between the Parliament, the Council and the Commission was complied with and, perhaps, what it entails. What is the result of non-compliance by the institutions with the deadlines laid down? What is the scope of the new provisions on economic and social cohesion, or research and technological development and, especially, on the environment? Has the Community taken action to ensure that environmental damage shall, as a priority, be rectified at source; what is the measure of compensation for polluters to pay and is that a national or a Community measure; what is the effect of providing that: ''Environmental protection requirements shall be a component of the Community's other policies?"[22] How far and in what circumstances can Member States avoid the harmonisation measures adopted under Article 100A on the grounds referred to in Article 36, or relating to protection of the environment or the working environment?

Whilst most of the "broadening versus deepening" argument has focused on the "deepening" aspect, it should not be forgotten that important developments having been taking place to broaden the Community, the most significant steps in this respect have been taken with regard to the EFTA states. For example, in September 1988, certain Member States of the Community and certain states of EFTA concluded the Lugano Convention on Jurisdiction and the Enforcement of Judgments in Civil and Commercial Matters,[23] the purpose of which is to ensure free movement of judgments in civil and commercial matters throughout both the EEC and the EFTA states. The Lugano Convention takes as a model the 1968 Brussels Convention, as amended, and essentially extends the provisions of this latter Convention to embrace an area which ultimately will comprise all the EEC Member States and the EFTA states.

Far more radical, however, is the proposed treaty to establish the European Economic Area (EEA) between the Community, its Member States and the EFTA states together with Liechtenstein. The agreement plans, broadly speaking, to create an area embracing the EEC Member States and the EFTA states in which provisions relating to the free movement of goods, persons, services and capital and to competition apply, all of which will be

---

[22] Article 130r(2) of the Treaty, as added by Article 25 of the Single European Act.
[23] O.J. L.319, p. 9.

closely based on the relevant provisions in the Treaty of Rome. The agreement will not, however, extend the common agricultural policy or the EEC customs union to the 19-member economic area.

In addition to the substantive provisions of the agreement, the question arose as to what machinery if any was necessary in order to deal with problems and disputes arising in the EFTA Member States (which do not have institutions comparable to those of the Community) and to deal with disputes which may involve both EFTA and EEC Member States.

Leaving aside all political considerations, it would obviously have been simpler from the jurisdictional point of view for the EFTA countries to accede individually to the Treaty of Rome, each accepting the existing structures and the jurisdiction of the European Court.

This is not, however, the chosen route and the question arises as to whether some form of judicial machinery is needed. There is no reason, in principle, why the European Court of Justice should not be bound by the decisions of some other court set up under a treaty adhered to by the Community. This would happen, for example, if the Community acceded to the European Convention on Human Rights. However, if effectively the broad basis of Community legislation is to be extended to the EFTA states, there are different considerations and the jurisdiction of the European Court has to be very carefully thought out.

It seemed clear from the beginning that if a judicial mechanism was to be adopted, the new court could not be simply the Court of Justice of the European Communities as it is now constituted. There is no reason why the EFTA countries should accept to be bound by the decisions of a court chosen by the Member States of the European Economic Community.

There were, however, many other possibilities.

One possibility might have been to have no court at all; another to have a court wholly separate from the European Court of Justice, which could apply a system of European Economic Area law, distinct from EEC law; another would have been to enlarge the European Court to include a representative of all the Member States of the European Free Trade Area; another would have been to adopt a system of international arbitration between the two bodies of EEC and EFTA. Finally (and this was the chosen solution), it was possible to envisage a court consisting of several (for example, five) members of the European Court of Justice and several (for example, three) members from the EFTA countries.

All these solutions present difficulties: of the relationship between the two systems of law; of the hierarchical position of the two courts if a second court is created; of the precedence of the judgments of one court over those of the other; of the status of the existing *acquis communautaire* as expressed in the judgments of the Court.

What seems to me to be crucial is that, unless the Member States of the European Economic Community decide to amend the Treaty of Rome (as it seems they have power to do), the legal order established for the Community itself should not be put in jeopardy by the structure adopted for this new European Economic Area. The European Court of Justice must, it seems to me, remain supreme whatever the procedure. I believe, too, that if any procedure for referring questions of law to the European Court of Justice is to be adopted, the Court's ruling should be binding on all the courts of the states involved. It seems to me that unless there is to be chaos, the *acquis communautaire* has to be accepted for the present and for the future. Legislation of the European Economic Community extended to the EFTA states must be construed by the European Court of Justice and applied in the same way throughout all the states party to the European Economic Area unless there are compelling reasons in the context of the appropriate legislation for adopting a different interpretation for the EFTA countries.

These are major problems, which are not only of political interest but which have considerable interest for lawyers. They go very much to the heart of the question as to what is the ultimate role of the European Court.

But this is only part of the future. Even leaving aside discussions with EFTA, it is clear that there are now five applications for full membership—from Austria and Sweden, Cyprus, Malta and Turkey. Others are likely to follow and already there is talk of a Community of 24 or even 30 members.

No less imminent are the close association agreements with Central European countries—Czechoslovakia, Poland, Hungary to name only three—the adoption of which, as a prelude to eventual accession, will no doubt produce questions for the Court as did the agreements with Greece and Portugal. The nature of these problems may juridically be no different in the future than in the past but an increase in volume is inevitable.

It is easy to enthuse about a solid bloc of European countries which satisfy the necessary democratic and human rights conditions, whose economies are capable of adjusting to the Community's aims and standards, and which accept the *acquis communautaire*. But the practical effects, not just for the Commission, the Council and the Parliament, but also for the Court, have to be kept in the forefront of our thinking.

The time is rapidly coming, if it has not already arrived, when a radical examination and rethink of, and not a mere tinkering with, the structure of the Court, of its jurisdiction and its procedures is needed.

An obvious first question for the future will relate to the size of the Court. It may be at first sight shocking to suggest that the Court may not be able to have one judge for each Member State. However, the fact that the United States Supreme Court does not have one judge from each state and that the Council of the new European Bank for Reconstruction does not have a member from each member state means that the question has to be asked, whatever the answer. And there are lots of other questions besides. I do not think that this examination is a task for members of the Court alone, although they should have the primary role. It is a task which needs the participation of a group, including representatives of senior judges, administrations and academic lawyers from the Member States as well as members of the Court.

This said, there seems to me no doubt that, even if taking decisions by majority voting and agreeing an increased competence for the Parliament reduces the need for judicial activism or creativity (which I doubt), the role of the Court will remain pivotal in holding the balance between institutions, in upholding the rule of law, in ensuring that the citizen's rights are protected and in keeping Member States to their commitments.

Jurisprudentially the next decade could be even more remarkable, indeed intellectually more exciting, than the past three decades.

There is no doubt that the depth and breadth of the European Court's influence in English Law, as in that of the legal system of the other Member States will increase. Whether Miss Hamlyn would have approved of the changes no one can know; it is in my view certain that she would have wished that they should be observed and studied not just by lawyers but by the people whose lives will be increasingly influenced by them.

CLOSING THOUGHT

"Quand la vapeur sera perfectionnée, quand, unie au télégraphe et aux chemins de fer, elle aura fait disparaître les distances, ce ne seront plus seulement les marchandises qui voyageront, mais encore les idées rendues à l'usage de leurs ailes. Quand les barrières fiscales et commerciales auront été abolies entre les divers États, comme elles le sont déjà entre les provinces d'un même État; quand les différents pays en relations journalières tendront à l'unité des peuples, comment ressusciterez-vous l'ancien mode de séparation?"

Chateaubriand, "Mémoires d'outre-tombe," 1841.

TABLE OF CASES

AM & S Europe *v.* Commission (Case 155/79) [1982] E.C.R. 1575 .... 34, 71

Administration des Douanes *v.* Gondrad Frères (Case 169/80) [1981]
E.C.R. 1931 37

Adoui and Cornuaille (Cases 115 & 116/81) [1982] E.C.R. 1665 108

Ählström and Others ("the *Woodpulp* case") (Cases 89, 104, 114,
116, 117 & 125–129/85) [1988] E.C.R. 5193 .... 64, 65

Ahmed Saeed Flugreisen (Case 66/86) [1989] E.C.R. 803 69

Akzo Chemie BV (Case 53/85) [1986] E.C.R. 1965 71

—— (Case C–62/86) Judgment of July 3, 1991 66

Alten and Hanburys Ltd. *v.* Generics (Case 113/80) [1988] E.C.R.
1245 50

Amsterdam Bulb (Case 50/76) [1977] E.C.R. 137 24

Antonissen (Case C–292/89) Judgment of February 26, 1991 94

Aragonesa de Publicidad Exterior (Cases 1 & 176/90) 51

Asjes (Cases 209–213/84) [1986] E.C.R. 1425 68

Association de Soutien aux Gravailleurs immigrés (Case C–213/90)
Judgment of July 4, 1991 104

Barber *v.* Guardian Royal Exchange Assurance Group (Case C–262/
88) [1990] E.C.R. I–1889 .... 121, 122, 125, 126, 127

Béguelin Import (Case 22/71) [1971] E.C.R. 949 63

Delhell (Case 246/81) [1982] E.C.R. 2277 68

Biehl (Case C–175/88) [1990] E.C.R. I–1779 103

Bilka-Kaufhaus (Case 170/84) [1986] E.C.R. 1607 122

Black Clawsol *v.* Papierwerke [1975] 1 All E.R. 810 42

Blaizot *v.* University of Liège (Case 24/86) [1988] E.C.R. 379 131

Blaupunkt-Werke GmbH (Case 245/87) [1989] E.C.R. 573 76

Bonchereau (Case 30/77) [1977] E.C.R. 1999 107

Bresciani (Case 87/75) [1976] E.C.R. 129 82

British American Tobacco and Reynolds *v.* Commission (Cases 142
& 156/84) [1987] E.C.R. 4487 70

British Beef Company *v.* Intervention Board of Agricultural
Produce (Case 146/77) [1978] E.C.R. 1347 37

Brown *v.* Secretary of State for Scotland (Case 197/86) [1988] E.C.R.
    3205 .... 103, 129, 132
Bulk Oil *v.* Sun International (Case 174/84) [1986] E.C.R. 559 .. 24, 79, 80

Campus Oil Ltd. (Case 72/83) [1984] E.C.R. 2727 52
Carmina di Leo *v.* Land Berlin (Case 308/89) [1990] E.C.R. 4185 130
Castelli (Case 261/83) [1984] E.C.R. 3199 103
Centrafarm *v.* Sterling Drug (Case 15/74) [1974] E.C.R. 1147 54
—— *v.* Winthrop (Case 16/74) [1974] E.C.R. 1183 55
Charmasson (Case 48/74) [1974] E.C.R. 1383 60
Cinéthèque SA *v.* Fédération nationale des cinémas français (Cases
    60–61/84) [1985] E.C.R. 2605 51
Coloroll Pension Trustees Ltd. *v.* Russell and Others (Case C–200/
    91) Reference from High Court 126
Commercial Solvents (Cases 6 & 7/73) [1974] E.C.R. 223 64
Commissaires réunis *v.* Receveur des douanes (Cases 80 & 81/77)
    [1978] E.C.R. 927 60
Commission *v.* Belgium (Case 149/79) [1980] E.C.R. 3881 & [1982]
    E.C.R. 1845 109
—— *v.* Council (Case 22/70) [1971] E.C.R. 263 78
—— *v.* —— (Case 45/86) [1987] E.C.R. 1493 24
—— *v.* —— (Case 131/87) [1989] E.C.R. 3764 27
—— *v.* —— (Case 242/87) [1989] E.C.R. 1425 134
—— *v.* —— (Case C–300/89) Judgment of June 11, 1991 .... 27, 28
—— *v.* Denmark (Case 302/86) [1988] E.C.R. 4627 .... 36, 51
—— *v.* France (Case 167/73) [1974] E.C.R 359 101
—— *v.* —— (Case 68/76 [1977] E.C.R. 515 60
—— *v.* —— (Case 96/85) [1986] E.C.R. 1475 120
—— *v.* —— (Case 307/84) [1986] E.C.R. 1725 109
—— *v.* Germany (Case 178/84 [1987] E.C.R. 1227 47
—— *v.* —— (Case C–57/89R) [1989] E.C.R. 2849 38
—— *v.* —— (Case C–195/90R) [1990] E.C.R. I–2715 39
—— *v.* Ireland (Case 61/77) [1978] E.C.R. 417 79
—— *v.* —— (Case 113/80) [1981] E.C.R. 1625 .... 49, 50
—— *v.* Italy (Case 24/68) [1969] E.C.R. 193 46
—— *v.* —— (Case 319/81) [1983] E.C.R. 601 45
—— *v.* —— (Case 225/85) [1987] E.C.R. 2625 109
—— *v.* —— (Case 63/86) [1988] E.C.R. 29 103
—— *v.* —— (Case C–235/89) Judgment of February 18, 1992 58
—— *v.* Netherlands (Case C–68/89) Judgment of May 30, 1991 96
—— *v.* United Kingdom (Case 246/89) [1989] E.C.R. 3125 20
—— *v.* —— (Case C–30/90) Judgment of February 18, 1992 58
Commissioner of Customs and Excise *v.* Ap Samex (Case 34/83)
    Judgment of January 29, 1984 11

Continental Can (Case 6/72) [1973] E.C.R. 215 64
Control Data Belgium (Case 294/81) [1983] E.C.R. 911 76
Costa *v.* ENEL (Case 6/64) [1964] E.C.R 1143 .... 15, 143
Costanzo (Case 103/88) [1989] E.C.R. 1839 17
Cotter and McDermott *v.* Minister for Social Welfare and Attorney
    General (Case 286/85) [1987] E.C.R. 1453 152
—— *v.* —— (Case 377/89) Judgment of March 13, 1991 152
Cowan (Case 186/87) [1989] E.C.R. 195 110

Danfoss (Case 109/88) [1989] E.C.R. 3199 .... 126, 127
Dassonville (Case 8/74) [1974] E.C.R. 837 47
Dechmann (Case 154/177) [1978] E.C.R. 1563 60
De Costa (Cases 28–30/62) [1963] E.C.R. 61 13
Defrenne *v.* Sabena (Case 43/75) [1986] E.C.R. 455 .... 122, 125
Demirel (Case 12/86) [1987] E.C.R. 3719 .... 79, 82
Denmark *v.* Commission (Case 171/78) [1980] E.C.R. 447 45
Diamanfarbeiders *v.* Indiamex (Cases 37 & 38/73) [1973] E.C.R.
    1609 75
Diatta (Case 267/83) [1986] E.C.R. 567 98
Donckerwolcke (Case 41/76) [1976] E.C.R. 1921 24
Drake *v.* Chief Adjudication Officer (Case 150/85) [1986] E.C.R.
    1995 20

Edeka (Case 245/81) [1982] E.C.R. 2745 74
Emmott *v.* Minister for Social Welfare and Attorney General (Case
    208/90) Judgment of July 25, 1991 .... 152, 153

Factortame *v.* Secretary of State for Transport (Case C–213/89) [1990]
    E.C.R. I–2433 .... 16, 19, 20
Faust (Case 52/81) [1982] E.C.R. 3745 75
Fiorini (Case 32/75) [1975] E.C.R. 1085 103
Foglia *v.* Novello (Case 244/80) [1981] E.C.R. 3066 22
—— *v.* —— (No.2) (Case 244/80) [1981] E.C.R. 3945 149
Foster *v.* British Gas (Case C–188/89) [1990] E.C.R. I–3313 124
—— *v.* —— [1991] 2 All E.R. 705 12
Foto-Frost *v.* Hauptzollamt Lübeck-Ost (Case 314/85) [1987] E.C.R.
    4199 13
France *v.* Commission (Case 168/78) [1980] E.C.R. 347 45
—— *v.* —— (Case C–22/90) Judgment of November 7, 1991 141
—— *v.* United Kingdom (Case 141/78) [1979] E.C.R. 2923 32
Francovich and Bonifaci (Cases C–6 & C–9/90) Judgment of Novem-
    ber 19, 1991 154
—— *v.* Italy (Cases 6 & 9/90) Judgment of November 19, 1991 17

GAEC de la Ségaude *v.* Council and Commission (Case 253/84)
    [1987] E.C.R. 123 61
Galli (Case 31/74) [1975] E.C.R. 45 60
Garland *v.* British Railways Board (Case 12/84) [1982] E.C.R. 555 121
Germany and others *v.* Commission (Case 281/85) [1987] E.C.R.
    3203 28
Gestetner Holdings (Case C–156/87) [1990] E.C.R. I–781 83
Geflügelschlachterei Freystadt (Case 23/79) (1979) E.C.R. 2789 80
Glocken GmbH and Kritzinger *v.* USL Centro sud et Provincia
    Autonome di Bolzano (Case 407/85) [1988] E.C.R. 4233 47
Gravier *v.* City of Liège (Case 293/83) [1985] E.C.R. 593 131
Groener (Case 379/87) [1989] E.C.R. 3967 104

Haegeman (Case 181/73) [1974] E.C.R. 449 79
Hilti *v.* Commission (Case T–30/89) [1990] E.C.R. II–163 71
Hinz *v.* Berry [1970] 2 Q.B. 41, C.A. 161
Hoechst *v.* Commission (Cases 46/87 & 227/88) [1989] E.C.R. 2919 .... 34, 71
Hoeckx (Case 249/83) [1985] E.C.R. 973 103
Hoffman La Roche (Case 102/77) [1978] E.C.R. 1139 54

Immigration Appeal Tribunal *v.* Mr. S. Singh (Case C–370/90)
    Judgment pending 99
Imperial Chemical Industries ("the *Dyestuffs* case") (Case 48/69)
    [1972] E.C.R. 619 64
Industrie Diensten Groep *v.* Beele (Case 6/81) [1982] E.C.R. 1625 51
International Fruit Company (Case 41-44/70) [1971] E.C.R. 436 83
—— (Cases 21–24/72) [1992] E.C.R. 1219 .... 80, 81
Italy *v.* Commission (Case 169/78) [1980] E.C.R. 385 45
—— *v.* —— (Case 303/88) Judgment of March 21, 1991 141
—— *v.* —— (Case 305/89) Judgment of March 21, 1991 141

Kempf (Case 139/85) [1986] E.C.R. 1741 90
Klopp (Case 107/83) [1984] E.C.R. 2971 120
Knoors (Case 115/78) (1979) E.C.R. 399 92
Könecke *v.* Balm (Case 117/83) [1984] E.C.R. 3291 37
Kayo Seiko (Case 256/84) [1987] E.C.R. 1899 83
Kramer (Case 3, 4 & 6/76) [1976] E.C.R. 1279 79
Kühlhaus-Zentrum *v.* Hauptzollant Hamburg-Harburg (Case 79/77)
    [1978] E.C.R. 611 61
Kupferberg (Case 104/81) [1982] E.C.R. 3641 82
Kowalska *v.* Freie und Hansestatd Hamburg (Case C–33/89) [1990]
    E.C.R. I–2591 121

Lair *v.* University of Hannover (Case 39/86) [1988] E.C.R.
    3161 .... 103, 129, 130

Lawrie-Blum (Case 66/85) [1986] E.C.R. 2121 88
Law Society of Upper Canada *v.* Skapinter [1984] 1 S.C.R. 357 21
Levin (Case 53/81) [1982] E.C.R. 1035 .... 90, 91
Lothar Messner (Case C–265/88) [1989] E.C.R. 4209 95
Luisi and Carbone (Cases 266/82 & 26/83([1984] E.C.R. 377 96

Marbury *v.* Madison 5 U.S. (1 Cranch) 137 .... 14, 21
Marleasing *v.* La Comercial Internacional de Alimentacion (Case
    C–106/89) [1990] E.C.R. I–4135 124
Marshall *v.* Southampton and South West Hampshire Health
    Authority (Case 152/84) [1986] E.C.R. 723 .... 16, 123
Martin *v.* Hunter's Lessee 14 U.S. (1 Wheat) 304 .... 14, 15, 22
Matteucci *v.* Communauté Française de Belgique (Case 235/87)
    [1988] E.C.R. 5585 129
Mauridis *v.* Parliament (Case 289/81) [1983] E.C.R. 1731 37
Meijer *v.* Department of Trade (Case 117/78) [1979] E.C.R. 1387 60
Merck Stephan (Case 187/80) [1981] E.C.R. 2063 54
Merkur *v.* Commission (Case 97/76) [1977] E.C.R. 1063 37
Michelin *v.* Commission (Case 322/82) [1983] E.C.R. 3461 .... 66, 72
Minebea (Case 260/84) [1987] E.C.R. 1975 83
Miro B.V. (Case 182/84) [1985] E.C.R. 3731 48
Morson and Jhanjan (Cases 35 & 36/82) [1982] E.C.R. 3723 99
Moser (Case 180/83) [1984] E.C.R. 2539 91
Musik-Vertrieb Membran and K-tel (Cases 55 & 57/80) [1981] E.C.R.
    147 55
Mutsch (Case 137/84) [1985] E.C.R. 2681 103

NTN Toyo Bearing Co. Ltd. (Case 113/77) [1979] E.C.R. 1185 74
—— (Case 240/84) [1987] E.C.R. 1809 83
Nachi Fujikoshi (Case 255/84) [1987] E.C.R. 1861 83
Nashua (Cases C–133 & C–150/87) [1990] E.C.R. I–719 83
Nederlandse Spoorwegen (Case 38/75) [1975] E.C.R. 1439 81
Norddeutsches Vieh und Fleischkontor (Case 14/74) [1974] E.C.R.
    899 80

Onnasch (Case 155/84) [1985] E.C.R. 1449 76
Orkem *v.* Commission (Case 374/87) [1989] E.C.R. 3283 .... 34, 72

Pabst und Richarz (Case 17/81) [1982] E.C.R. 1331 82
Parke Davis (Case 24/67) [1968] E.C.R. 55 54
Parliament *v.* Council (Case 13/83) [1985] E.C.R. 1513 29
—— *v.* —— (Case 302/87) [1988] E.C.R. 5615 30
—— *v.* —— (Case 70/88) [1990] E.C.R. I–2024 30
—— *v.* —— (Case C–295/90) Judgment pending 133

Patrick (Case 11/77) (1977) E.C.R. 1199 116
Pharmon (Case 19/84) (1985) E.C.R. 2281 54
Pieck (Case 157/79) (1980) E.C.R. 2171 95
Prantl (Case 16/83) [1984] 1299 48
Prodest (Case 237/83) [1984] E.C.R. 3153 72
Pronuptia de Paris *v.* Schillgalis (Case 161/84) [1986] E.C.R. 353 .... 69, 70

R. *v.* Ministry of Agriculture, Fisheries and Food *ex parte* Fedesa
    (Case 331/88) [1990] E.C.R. 4057 36
Rau *v.* De Smedt (Case 261/81) [1982] E.C.R. 3961 48
Raulin *v.* Dutch Minister of Education and Science (Case C–357/89)
    Judgment pending 130, 132, 133
Reed (Case 59/85) [1986] E.C.R. 1283 98
Reina (Case 65/81) [1982] E.C.R. 33 103
Rewe-Zentrale AG (Case 120/78) [1979] E.C.R. 649 .... 47, 50
Royer (Case 48/75) [1976] E.C.R. 497 93
Ryborg (Case C–297/89) Judgment of April 23, 1991 110

SA CNL-Sucal NV *v.* Hag (Case C–10/89) [1990] E.C.R. I–3711 56
SAFA (Case C–337/88) [1990] E.C.R. I–1 37
SARL Aliments Morvan (Case C–235/90) Judgment of November 19,
    1991 61
SIOT (Case 266/81) [1983] E.C.R. 731 46
SPI and SAMI (Cases 267–269/81) [1983] E.C.R. 801 .... 81, 84
Simmenthal (Case 35/76) [1976] E.C.R. 1871 13
—— (Case 106/77) [1978] E.C.R. 629 16
Sirena (Case 40/70) [1971] E.C.R. 69 .... 54, 55
The Society for the Protection of Unborn Children Ireland Ltd.
    v. Grogan and others (Case C–159/90) Judgment of October 4,
    1991 35
Sotrimport *v.* Commission (Case C–152/88) [1990] E.C.R. 2504 33
Solvay *v.* Commission (Case 27/88) [1989] E.C.R. 3355 72
Sotgiu *v.* Deutsche Bundespost (Case 152/73) [1974] E.C.R. 153 102
Stauder (Case 11/70) [1970] E.C.R. 1125 at 1134 34
Stichting Collective Antennevoorziening Gouda and others
    v. Conissariaat voor de Media (Case C–288/89) Judgment of
    July 25, 1991 .... 52, 53
Suiker Unie and others *v.* Commission (Cases 40–48, 50, 54–56, 111,
    113 and 114/73) [1975] E.C.R. 1663 60
Syndicat général des fabricants de semoules de France [1970]
    C.M.L.R. 395 19

Technische Universität München (Case C–269/70) Judgment of
    November 21, 1991 76

Terrapin (Case 119/75) [1976] E.C.R. 1039 55
Thieffry (Case 71/76) [1977] E.C.R. 765 .... 115, 116

UNECTEF v. Heylens (Case 222/86) [1987] E.C.R. 4097 102
United Brands (Case 27/76) [1978] E.C.R. 207 .... 65, 66
United Kingdom (Case 170/78) [1980] E.C.R. 417 45
—— v. Commission (Case 61/86) [1988] E.C.R. 431 60
—— v. Council (Case 68/86) [1988] E.C.R. 857 29
United Kingdom, France and Germany v. Council (Case C–51, C–90
   & C–94/89) Judgment of June 11, 1991 134
—— v. —— (Comet II) (Cases C–51, 90 & 94/89) [1992] 1 C.M.L.R.
   40 29

Van den Hazel (Case 111/76) [1977] E.C.R. 901 24
Van Duyn (Case 41/74) [1974] E.C.R. 1337 107
Van Gend en Loos (Case 26/62) [1963] E.C.R. 3 16
Van Zuyten v. Hag (Case 192/73) [1974] E.C.R. 731 56
Von Colson (Case 14/83) [1984] E.C.R. 1891 124

Watson and Belmann (Case 118/75) [1976] E.C.R. 1185 95
Webb (Case 279/80) [1981] E.C.R. 3305 53
Windsurfing International (Case 193/83) [1986] E.C.R. 611 54

Züchner (Case 172/80) [1981] E.C.R. 2021 68
Zwartfeld (Case C–2/88) [1990] E.C.R. 1–3365 10

TABLE OF TREATIES

1957 Treaty Establishing the European Economic Community (E.E.C.) (March 25, 1957) 7, 43, 46, 55, 57
Art. 2 60
Art.3 (1) 86
Art. 5 ... 9, 115, 117, 119
Art. 7 .... 20, 111, 131, 133
Art. 12 .... 45, 47
Art. 30 ... 45, 47, 50, 53, 54, 58, 59
Art. 34 47
Art. 36 ... 49, 50, 51, 53, 54, 168
Art. 40 35
Art. 43 29
Art. 48 ... 86, 87, 88, 89, 91, 92, 93, 94, 100, 101
(2) 101
(3) 107
(4) 109
Art. 49 92
Art. 52 ..... 20, 113, 114, 115, 117, 119
Art. 56 52
Art. 57 115
Art. 59 .... 35, 113
Art. 84 68
Art. 85 ... 34, 63, 69, 70, 72, 145, 151

1957 Treaty Establishing the European Economic Community (E.E.C.) —cont.
Art. 86 ... 34, 63, 65, 69, 72, 145, 151
Art. 95 45
Art. 100A ... 27, 28, 168
Art. 110 73
Art. 113 .. 73, 78, 80, 84
Art. 119 . 120, 121, 122, 123, 125, 127
Art. 128 .... 29, 131, 133
Art. 130R 24
(2) 168
(4) 25
Art. 130S 27, 28
Art. 149 133
Art. 164 34
Art. 168A 139
Art. 169 ..... 22, 32, 147, 148, 151, 152
Art. 170 31
Art. 173 ..... 21, 30, 143, 166
Art. 175 ...... 29, 30, 144
Art. 177 ... 9, 18, 21, 22, 29, 68, 79, 81, 125, 127, 142, 143, 144, 145, 149, 154, 165
Art. 178 33
Art. 189 123
Art. 219 31

1957 Treaty Establishing
  the European
  Economic Com-
  munity
  (E.E.C.) (March
  25, 1957)—*cont.*
  Art. 222 54
  Art. 228 78
  Art. 229–231 78
  Art. 235 112,
       133, 134
  Art. 236 74
  Art. 238 78
  Title III 120
  Title III, Chap. 2 . 113

1957 Protocol on the Sta-
  tute of the
  Court of Justice
  of the European
  Community—
  Art. 51 .... 163, 165
  Art. 52 163
  Art. 54 164
1987 Single European Act
  (O.J. 1987, No.
  L169/1) 146
  Art. 11 139
  Art. 25 168

INDEX

Agricultural Policy,
  monetary compensation, 61
  national organisation, 60
  obstacles to free movement, 60
  operation, 59–60
Air Transport,
  competition rules, 68–69
Australia,
  Constitution,
    judicial review, power, 21
    states' competence, 23
    supremacy of
        Commonwealth, 15
  federal system, 7–8, 9
  High Court's role, 30–31
  individuals' rights, 33

Canada,
  Constitution,
    provinces' competence, 23
    supremacy, 15
  federal system, 7–8
  individuals' rights, 33
  judicial review, power, 21
  Supreme Court's role, 30–31
Common Market,
  agricultural policy, 59–61
  charges resembling customs,
    45–46
    definition, 46
  competition rules,
    abuse of dominant position,
      63, 65–68
    application, 68–71

Common Market—*cont.*
  competition rules—*cont.*
    financial considerations, 66
    geographical extent of
      Court's jurisdiction,
      63–65
    lifting veil, 63–64
    necessity, 62–63
    predatory pricing, 66
    price competition, 66–68
    restrictive practices,
      62–63
  creation,
    generally, 44
    overturning barriers, 44–48,
      62–63
      exceptions, 48–53
  equivalence principle, 47–48
    exceptions, 49–53
  free movement, 61–62
  interllectual property cases,
    58–59
  international trade. *See*
    International Trade.
  measures resembling import
    restrictions, 45–48
    definition, 47
  national laws,
    disparities between, 50
    mandatory requirements,
      50–53
  procedures, 71–73
  protection of property rights,
    Court's position, 54–55

Common Market—*cont.*
  protection of property rights—
    cont.
    exhaustion of rights theory,
      54–55
    problems, 54
    relationship with free
      movement of goods,
      55
  taxes, discrimination, 44–45
  trade marks, 55–58
Community,
  adjudication,
    necessity, 6–9
    system adopted, 9
  applications for full
    membership, 171
  broadening, 168
  Central Europe, close association
    agreements, 171
  doubts regarding, 2
  federal system,
    differences from, 7–8
    non-adoption, 6–7
  institutions. *See* **Institutions of
    Community.**
  interest in, 2
Court of First Instance,
  appeal against decision,
    163–166
  creation, 139, 146–147
    practical effects, 145
  precedents, 165–166
  relationship with Court of
    Justice, 162–166
  workload, 140–144
Court of Justice,
  administrative discussions,
    158–160
  answering references, 149–150
  change, need for, 137–138,
    144–145
  contribution to European
    integration, 43–44

Court of Justice—*cont.*
  declarations, validity of acts of
    Community institutions,
    12–13
  delays, 137
  development, 136–137
  effectiveness. *See* **Effectiveness
    of Court of Justice.**
  effects doctrine, 64
  evidence, consideration, 166
  features, 41
  final arbiter, 146
  GATT,
    interpretation, 83–84
    judicial review, 83–84
    jurisdiction, 81, 83
  generally, 39–40
  interim relief, 37–39
  international position, 73–77,
    84
  interpretation of Community
    legislation, 42–43
  judgment,
    dissenting, 161–162
    enforcement, 151–152
    hammering out, 158,
      160–161
    State's failure to comply
      with, 149, 150–151
    style, 160–161
  jurisdiction,
    appellate, 163–166
    EFTA Member States,
      169–171
    scope, 138–147
  oral argument, limitation of time,
    154–155
  position, 3
  preparation of case, 155–156
  presentation of documents,
    155
  procedures,
    alteration, 147–149, 157–160
    "fast track," 154

Court of Justice—*cont.*
procedures—*cont.*
  United States Supreme
      Court contrasted, 160
  questions of Community law,
      calling in, 10
    refusal, 12
  radical examination necessary,
      171–172
  relationship with Court of First
      Instance, 162–166
  role, 3, 30–31, 172
    ultimate, 171
  Single Market legislation,
      167–168
  size, 172
  staff cases,
    proposal for tribunal,
        138–139
    resolution, 145–146
    Tribunal. *See* **Court of First
        Instance.**
Customs Union, 44

Defence's Rights,
  safeguarding, 72–73
Dublin Convention, 113

EFTA Member States, 168–169
Effectiveness of Court of Justice,
  conflict with national law, 14
  direct effectiveness, 16, 18
  hierarchy of norms, 14, 18
  interpretation of Community
      legislation, 13, 42–43
  judicial reviewing power,
    acts of institutions, 21–22
    national measures, 22–23
  relationship between
      Community law and
      national law, 15–19
  supremacy, 16, 18–19
Equal Opportunities Commission,
  128

**Equality between Men and
    Women,**
  burden of proof, 126–127
  Court's approach, 121
  direct effect of Article 119,
      122–123
  directives' horizontal direct
      effect, 123–125
  discrimination, 120–121
  limitation of effects of Court's
      judgments, 125–126
  necessity on economic grounds,
      120
  pay, 120–123
  pensions, 121–122
  State body employers, 124–125
  transparency, 126–127
  treatment directive, 123
  value directive, 123
European Economic Area, 168–169,
  170

FEOGA cases, 141
Franchising, 69–70

Germany,
  federal system, 7, n.4
  individuals' rights, 34

Individuals,
  damages,
    claims, 33
    guidelines, 152
    State's failure to transpose
        directive, 17–18,
        151–154
  direct actions before Court, 32–33
  drug carriers, 97, 109–110
  education, 128–134
    discrimination, 131–132
  effects of Community, 85–86
  equality between men and
      women. *See* **Equality
      between Men and Women.**

Individuals—*cont.*
  freedom of movement,
    compensation for harm,
      110–111
    directives, 111–112
    generally, 109
    harmonisation of laws,
      112–113
    problems, 109–110
  legal certainty, 37
  legitimate expectations,
    36–37
  proportionality, 36
  reasonableness, 36
  retroactive measures, 37
  rights under Community law,
    fundamental rights, 34
    generally, 33
    scope, 34–35
  security risk, 96, 109–110
  students,
    COMET programme, 134
    ERASMUS programme, 134
    grants, 131–132
    residence for foreigners,
      132–134
    rights under Community
      law, 128–131
  workers. *See* **Workers.**
Institutions of Community,
  inter se, 27–31
  Member States' position. *See*
    Member States, institutions
    of Community.
  need for,
    majority decision, 27–28
    unanimous decision, 27–28
  voting by majority, 28–29
International Trade,
  agreements, international,
    commercial policy, 79
    Community's power to
      enter into, 77–79
    implied, 78–79

International Trade—*cont.*
  agreements, international—*cont.*
    limitation of Member State's
      powers, 78, 79
    political issues, 79–80
  common customs tariff, 75–76
  dumping, protection against, 77
  General Agreement on Tariffs
    and Trade (GATT),
    Community's substitution
      for States, 80–81
    Court's jurisdiction, 81, 83
    effect in Community, 81–83
  generally, 73–74
Ireland,
  abortion prohibition, 35–36

Languages,
  interpretation, versions of
    legislation, 42–43
Lugano Convention, 168

Maastricht Conference,
  importance, 2
Member States,
  institutions of Community,
    environmental issues, 24–25
    relationship with, 23–24
    subsidiarity principle, 25–26
  inter se, 31–32
Mergers,
  control, 70–71

National,
  courts,
    disapproval of Court's
      decisions, 10–11
    references by, 9–10
    relationship with Court of
      Justice, 11–12, 15–16,
      22–23
  customs at Court of Justice, 4–5
  laws, mandatory requirements,
    50–53
  legal systems, 5–6

1992,
approach, 1–2

Object of Author, 3
Outlook,
author's, 4
in United Kingdom, 4

Parliament, European,
declaration, application to Court
for, 29–30
interventions by, 29
judicial review, 29
People. *See* **Individuals.**
Professions,
free movement,
Court's case law, 114–120
interference with, 96
qualifications necessary, 113
removal of difficulties, 114
freedom of establishment,
115–116
lawyers, 118–119
secrecy, professional, 71

Schengen Agreement, 112–113
Search and Seizure, 71–72
Self-incrimination, 72
Services,
establishment and provision, 113
Social Charter, 134–135
Subsidiarity Principle, 25–26

Treaty of Rome,
Article 5, 9–10
features, 41
judicial review, power, 21
policy sections, 62
States' competence, 23
supremacy, 15

United Kingdom Law,
conflicts with Community law,
19–20
equal opportunity cases, 127–128

United Kingdom Law—*cont.*
interim injunction against
Crown, 16–17
patents, compulsory licences,
58
United States,
Constitution,
federal courts, 6
interpretation, 14–15
states' competence, 23
supremacy, 14–15
differences from European
Economic Community, 6–7
individuals' rights, 33
judicial review, power, 20–21
Supreme Court's role, 30–31

Workers,
equal treatment after move,
Court's influence,
101–107
covert discrimination,
102–104
generally, 100–101
judicial review, 102
overrriding reasons for
discriminination,
104–106
social and tax advantages,
102–103
social security, 106–107
family,
education, 129, 130
exercise of Community
rights by worker, 99
rights of members, 97–100
free movement,
Court's attitude, 92–97
date, 86–87
interference with, 94–97
legislation, 87
limitations, 107–109
proportionality, 107–109
meaning, 87, 88, 91–92

Workers—*cont.*
  free movement—*cont.*
    public service employees, 109
    temporary departure, 92
  looking for work, 92–94

Workers—*cont.*
  meaning, 88–89
  part-time, 89–91
  retired, right of residence, 99–100
  students, as, 128–130